Praise for *How to Have A Match Made in Heaven*
A Transformational Approach to Dating, Relating

"Hallelujah, a relationship book that makes sense! *How to Have A Match Made in Heaven* delivers simple yet powerful principles and grounded, real-life, believable examples of people who made huge progress in their relationships by loving and accepting themselves. I resonate deeply with the Kanes' teachings and know with absolute confidence that anyone who puts these ideas into practice is in for a richer, more rewarding love life. The linked videos provide a brilliant asset, bringing the individuals and couples to life. At a time when so many people struggle with relationships, this book can serve as a significant roadmap to connection with self and a perfect partner."
- Alan Cohen, author of *Don't Get Lucky, Get Smart*

"The most important relationship you will ever have is the one with yourself. The Kanes understand this, so they begin at the source working outward. Cultivating an understanding of the effect we have on ourselves, those around us and finally the world as a whole allows us to be an instrument for greater change. *How to Have A Match Made in Heaven* is an indispensable tool that should be on everyone's shelf, no matter your relationship status."
- Amit Goswami, Ph.D., theoretical physicist, acclaimed worldwide speaker, author of *How Quantum Activism Can Save Civilization*

"Honesty and communication are crucial to the success of any relationship and Ariel and Shya Kane are empowering people in every part of the world to enjoy thriving, enduring relationships by learning to be honest with themselves and those they love and improve communication skills. The tools and mindset strategies you will gain from these pages are timeless and highly effective; to invest in this book is to invest in your happiness for a lifetime."
- Ivan Misner, Ph.D., *New York Times* bestselling author and founder of BNI®

"From childhood, we are brainwashed by fairy tales about 'falling in love and living happily ever after.' With the help of Ariel and Shya Kane's book, you will learn how to retain that enthusiasm for love while being able to deal with the real-world problems every relationship is bound to encounter. They help you to better understand yourself and your actions, thus leading to a more complete picture of all the important relationships in your life."
- Betsey Chasse, filmmaker, co-creator of the hit documentary *What the BLEEP Do We Know!?*

"Everyone is looking for the kind of relationship the Kanes have. Some may be lucky enough to have already found it, but for anyone who is still searching, or still working at finding and creating a 'match made in heaven', this latest book from Ariel and Shya .... advice with real-life stories and examples to boost your co   ng for, and enhance your chances of finding th
- Stephen Gawtry, mai   *)Y SPIRIT Magazine*

D1091344

Praise for *How to Create A Magical Relationship: The 3 Simple Ideas That Will Instantaneously Transform Your Love Life*

2007 Nautilus Book Award: Winner, category of Relationships / Men & Women's Issues. *"...a profound journey into the world of relationships...filled with simple but powerful principles."*

2007 Eric Hoffer Award: Notable Winner, category of Health/Self-Help

2007 *ForeWord Magazine* Book of the Year Award:
Finalist, categories of Family & Relationships and Self-Help

"A masterpiece...unprecedented by any other relationship genre book this reviewer has ever come across."
- Awareness Magazine

"Years of therapy cannot touch what the Kanes can do in minutes...10 stars for this outstanding work."
- Dr. Maryel McKinley

"The secrets to magical and fulfilling relationships are all here – there's no need to look further."
- Stephen Gawtry, editor, *The Watkins Review*

"A fresh new approach to age old problems."
- New York Spirit Magazine

"...truly a masterpiece of the self-help genre that is destined to become the first 'line of defense' for troubled relationships."
- Mary A. Arsenault, publisher, *Wisdom Magazine*

"...you need to read this most incredible book that just might change the way you look at yourself, your partner, and yes – your relationship."
- *Inner Tapestry,* Maine's Holistic Journal

"A well-written book with lots of positive self-affirming directions and the first of the self-help books about living in the moment that effectively tackles the problem of relationships. This is a highly recommended book."
- Harold McFarland,
Readers Preference Reviews & *Midwest Book Review*

"The Kanes are really on to something. The book reads easily, not dancing around serious issues, and not getting bogged down in self-help vernacular."
- New York Resident Magazine

"Plenty of wisdom...plenty of gold"
- Kirkus Reviews

"Ariel and Shya Kane's book *How to Create a Magical Relationship* will help you create vital, supportive partnerships that flow smoothly day in and day out, not just when things are easy."
- *Nexus Magazine*

"...excellent...easy-to-read...a strong guide for those looking for direction in their relationships."
- *ForeWord Magazine*

Praise for *Working on Yourself Doesn't Work: The 3 Simple Ideas That Will Instantaneously Transform Your Life*

"Don't let the title mislead you. *Working on Yourself Doesn't Work* is not about the futility of self-improvement but rather about the effortlessness of transformation.... A simple, easy-to read book with a valuable message that can take you through the swamp of the mind into the clarity and brilliance of the moment."
- Kim Stevenson, *Whole Life Times Magazine*

"I strongly recommend this book. Ariel and Shya Kane are at the forefront in the field of personal transformation and have much to offer anyone who wants a more meaningful and fulfilling life."
- Paul English, publisher, *New York Spirit Magazine*

"#1 Best Book Buy. 10+! A 'must' for the library of every seeker of truth!"
- *Awareness Magazine*

#1 Best Seller in Self-Help/Personal Transformation & Satisfaction categories.
- Amazon.com

"This warm, accessible book will illuminate and befriend your transformation."
- Mary Nurrie Stearns, editor, *Personal Transformation Magazine*

"This book is a must read. One to have on your bookshelf and to share with your friends."
- *To Your Health Magazine*

"Ariel and Shya Kane actually 'walk the talk'.... This simple yet profound book teaches us how to live in the moment. *Working on Yourself Doesn't Work* is refreshing, truthful, sincere, and authentic and written with insightfulness and clarity."
- Dr. Maryel McKinley

"In an era of technological revolutions affecting how we work and how we communicate, the Kanes are creating a revolution in how we live."
- Andrew Gideon, vice president, TAG Online, Inc.

"As a physicist, I don't know how they do it, but my life has been transformed by being around the Kanes. When serious life events come up – prostate cancer, my son disabled by a brain tumor, losing a job due to downsizing – I have been able to remain on-center and engaged in my life, not a victim. The Kanes' approach to living has had a dramatic impact on my happiness and effectiveness. I highly recommend their seminars and their new book which explains their transformational technique to everyone."
- William R. Ellis, Ph.D., vice president, Advanced Technology, Raytheon

Praise for *Being Here: Modern Day Tales of Enlightenment*

"This little gem of a book injects all the 'how to' directly into the reader's bloodstream, engaging the imagination.... Its deceptively simple format – stories – cracks open amazing possibilities for transformation."
- *ForeWord Magazine*

"Prescription for the good life...recommended for public libraries... inspirational."
- *Library Journal*

"Astounding.... If you're looking for enlightenment, then you need look no further than this book."
- David Riklan, founder, SelfGrowth.com

"A must for every self-help book shelf!"
- Dr. Maryel McKinley

"This is a book of ordinary everyday moments, yet profound moments, helping us all navigate our daily experiences with the resonation of universal truths of the ages."
- *Inner Tapestry*

"An enlightened approach to the difficulties we all face in our life journey."
- *Wisdom Magazine*

"Ariel and Shya Kane have done it again in producing yet another masterpiece."
- *Love in Santa Fe Magazine*

"Sincerely helpful.... This book delivers."
- *New York Spirit Magazine*

Practical
Enlightenment

Ariel & Shya Kane

Waterfront Press

Library of Congress Cataloging-in-Publication Data

Kane, Ariel.
     Practical Enlightenment / by Ariel & Shya Kane.
     ISBN-13: 978-1-943625-01-7

     1. Self-help 2. Spirituality 3. Happiness

Listening and its Effect on Learning by Andrew Gideon
All Rights Reserved. Used by Permission.

Photo of Kanes by Terri Diamond
Cover photo by Ariel Kane.

For the folks on the

ACT team (American Community of Transformation)

and the ETC team (European Transformation Community)

who have supported us in bringing

transformation and Practical Enlightenment

to people around the world.

This one is for you.

CONTENTS

FOREWORD

Years ago, before I experienced transformation, I believed I was broken and it would take a lot of work to fix me. I also believed that there were certain parts of me – the nasty, twisted parts – that were beyond repair. I worked hard on myself, using self-criticism and self-help books, to try and change what I thought to be wrong, doing my best to hide the worst-beyond-repair parts. Needless to say, I lived a very painful life.

Then I discovered *Instantaneous Transformation*, the technology developed by Ariel and Shya Kane. I read their first book, *Working on Yourself Doesn't Work*, gobbling it up in just one sitting. Afterwards, I simply sat for a few hours, smiling to myself. I had absorbed the experience of transformation. I felt perfect, just the way I was. I wasn't worrying about the future or thinking about the past. I no longer wanted to change my life or meet my goals in order to be happier. I felt happy with everything, just the way it was. I didn't know how that could be true, but it was. I didn't understand it and I didn't need to.

Reading the Kanes' book opened up a portal of possibility in my life. I'd never felt so at peace with myself and I was curious to know what else was possible, so I signed up for their next workshop and flew from England to Hamburg, Germany, to experience transformation in person. Once again, on an even deeper level, I experienced the feeling of being perfect, just as I was. I hadn't done anything special. I hadn't spoken about what

I thought was wrong with me and my life. I simply sat in the workshop, listened, and I transformed.

Most of us believe there is something wrong with us. We see ourselves on a spectrum of failure that runs from "a little flawed" to "totally f**ked up." On our good days, we're a little flawed. On our bad days we're f**ked up beyond repair. We believe this and we tell ourselves (and other people) over and over again how and why this is true. We say it aloud and we say it silently. We speak these words and we listen to them every hour of every day of every year of our lives.

I spent nearly thirty years listening to what I believed was wrong with me. Then, one day, I stopped listening to those thoughts and started listening to something else instead. That's when my life transformed. That's when I experienced the magic of this moment of now. Ariel and Shya say that it doesn't matter what they talk about – they could read the phone book aloud – as long as you listen. When you listen to what is being said, you stop listening to your commentary of self-criticism. That is when your life transforms.

One of the ideas within *Instantaneous Transformation* is that no two things can occupy the same space at the same time. While you're listening to one thing, you can't simultaneously listen to another. When you're absorbing the words that someone else is saying, you cannot also listen to the words in your own head. Likewise, when you're fully engaged with anything you're doing, you can't be thinking those negative thoughts at the same time.

The first time I experienced transformation simply through listening, I was sitting on a bench one sunny Saturday afternoon in Hamburg, Germany, sharing lunch with a stranger I'd just met at one of the Kanes' weekend seminars. I was chatting away, telling her about myself, and then I asked her to tell me about herself. When she began, I tried to listen. I tried to let go of my thoughts, but I just kept thinking things like, "Perhaps I shouldn't have told her that. She'll think I'm an idiot. She'll think I'm arrogant. I wish I'd said something about . . ."

Suddenly, what Ariel and Shya had been saying during the seminar about listening clicked. They'd talked (as they do in all their seminars and at the beginning of every radio show) about how true listening is the gateway to being in the moment and when you're in the moment, your life transforms. I'd heard them and I'd understood it – as a concept. Then, in the next instant, I experienced it as reality.

That afternoon during lunch, I listened, really and truly – syllable-by-syllable, word-by-word, sentence-by-sentence, moment-by-moment. At first the commentary in my head chattered alongside everything this woman said. But gradually, as I kept bringing my attention to her words, my own thoughts subsided and soon my mind was empty. The roll call of self-criticism had vanished and I was simply sitting on a bench in the sunshine with a stranger, happier than I'd ever been. Nothing needed fixing or changing. Everything was perfect exactly as it was. I had thought the road to happiness was going to be a long, complex and painful one, full of angst as I attempted to mend all that I believed was broken in me. But in fact, it had been mind-blowingly simple, heart-opening and pain-free.

As long as you think there's something wrong with you, you act out those thoughts and turn them into reality. But the miracle is, when you stop listening to the commentary of self-criticism, you stop believing that you're all messed up. When you stop believing that you're all messed up, you stop acting as if you're all messed up. When you stop acting as if you're all messed up, you no longer are. When you stop listening to those thoughts, you act out your inner perfection and that becomes your reality instead. This doesn't take work or effort and it doesn't take time. One moment you're flawed and the next moment you're not. It's as simple and profound as that.

In this book, Ariel and Shya offer you the opportunity to experience transformation for yourself. I recommend that you read *Practical Enlightenment* in the same way you would read a fairy tale. Simply immerse yourself in the story. "Listen" to the words without applying anything as "advice" to fix yourself. This book isn't a pill to fix your flaws and make you perfect. It's a light to illuminate inside of you the natural knowing that you already are perfect, exactly as you are. When you experience that, you will experience enlightenment.

– Menna van Praag

PREFACE

In 1999 we self-published our first book, *Working on Yourself Doesn't Work*, which we subsequently expanded when it was republished by McGraw-Hill in 2008. All these years later, and after working with millions of people via our books, seminars and radio show, *Being Here*, it has become obvious that Working on Yourself *Still* Doesn't Work.

This book is not about the futility of self-help or self-introspection but rather about the effortlessness and effectiveness of Instantaneous Transformation – where you experience the perfection of this moment and ultimately your own perfection.

When you are really Being Here, not lost in your plans or worries about the future, or tangled up in thoughts about what you would have, could have or should have done, then your life becomes vibrant. You perceive yourself, your environment and the people around you in a profound way and life transforms into an exciting adventure in which every moment counts. When you are truly Being Here your life transforms in an instant and, practically speaking, you are enlightened.

In the following pages we share our own personal experiences and the experiences of many people in our transformational community who have generously allowed us to include their stories as well, for which we are deeply grateful. Enjoy the journey.

– Ariel & Shya Kane

1

THE ESSENTIAL SHIFT

The day the essential shift happened, it was a totally unexpected event. On that ordinary morning, nothing pointed to the fact that by the end of that day, our lives would be utterly different and that this shift would not only last but would expand throughout the rest of our lives.

It was 1987 and we had recently returned to the United States from Europe where we had been studying at The International Meditation Center. The last workshop we attended there had been a six-month intensive for twenty-four hours a day, seven days a week. Along with the other participants, we had been diligently working to transform our lives, striving to better ourselves so that we could reach a state of enlightenment.

The course was the culmination of years of study for us, both individually (Ariel was 29 and Shya was 46) and together as a couple. We were both passionate about moving beyond a mundane existence and we wanted to squeeze all the juice from life. We were always striving to get ahead and even when we were meditating, we had an underlying urge to compare how we were doing with those around us. We were in competition to be the best and we were always working: to quiet our minds, to be still within, to improve and to be better.

Prior to our stint at the meditation center, we'd engaged in years of self-introspection and self-growth seminars. We'd walked on hot coals, visualized our goals, changed our diets, made endless lists, and had tirelessly repeated affirmations, always trying to fix ourselves and those around us, hoping to find a sense of day-to-day well-being. We'd achieved success in our lives and careers. We'd bought a Park Avenue apartment in New York City, only to realize that we felt empty and devoid of any real sense of well-being. In a pendulum swing of tactics, we sold the apartment and most of our worldly goods and financed our two years at the meditation center, which was quite an expensive proposition. By the time we returned, our credit cards were maxed out, we were driving a car we borrowed from Ariel's parents and we were living in a rented room in someone's apartment in San Francisco, California. And still, we were striving to be enlightened.

Around this time, we attended yet another workshop offered by the folks who had run the meditation center in Italy. They had come to California to present their seminars and as we were sitting in the room, listening to them speak, we realized that if we jumped back into working on ourselves and each other, we were destined to undergo another round of pain and suffering. We suddenly knew that this path would lead to a never-ending treadmill of self-doubt and that this particular road was no longer one we wanted to take. Stumped about our next move and confused about what to do with our lives, we took a break.

One morning, lacking anything better to do, we decided to take a walk. We'd been reading from a book about a seventeenth century Zen master named Bankei who had attained enlightenment by sitting on a hard rock for twenty years. But once he became enlightened, he realized that sitting on that hard rock did not produce his enlightenment. We found this idea intriguing.

Stepping out the door of the apartment, we took a right turn and headed down the hill to the beach. We weren't going anywhere in particular that day. We were just enjoying the sunlight on our shoulders and the cool sea breeze on our faces. We were walking in tandem, in sync with ourselves and each other, not trying to get anywhere, simply being. Our route to the beach took us through a little park that was glowing bright orange from a profusion of poppies in the flowerbeds. When we arrived at the seashore, to our delight, a group of California sea lions was cavorting offshore, diving, playing and lounging on the rocks as families with small pups played in the surf.

Eventually we decided to head back up the hill to the apartment to prepare some lunch. Between one step and another, Shya fell. He didn't fall to the ground. He didn't fall to his knees. He fell directly into the moment – and in that moment, our lives instantaneously transformed. In an instant, he had a direct and profound experience that the moment was perfect and by extension, he discovered that he was perfect as well and that we were perfect, too. He recognized that working on himself or on us was denying the perfection of the moment. Here is the conversation that followed:

"Ariel, I'm living consistent with the manner Bankei describes in the book we're reading," Shya said. "I'm enlightened."

"You can't say that. People will hate you," Ariel replied.

"I don't care," Shya stated. "It's the truth. It's my truth."

In that moment Shya stopped picking on himself and he stopped working on Ariel in his thoughts. As he turned to look at Ariel, there was something new in him, a calm, quiet strength. There was serenity. A click happened between us.

"OK," Ariel said. "I see it now."

We continued up the hill and went on with our lives. We still didn't know what was next but we knew we were finished working on ourselves and on each other and were content to see how life unfolded.

Shortly afterward, we returned to the New York City area. Coming full circle, we stayed in our old Park Avenue apartment that the new owner briefly loaned to us while he was out of town. Walking down the street one day, we ran into an old friend who had known us throughout our arduous journey from workshop to workshop.

"You're so different," he said. "You're so...here. It's obviously the real thing! What are you doing now?"

"Nothing," Shya said. "We're just living our lives."

"Wow," the man said, "this is important. I'd like you to come speak with my company and I'll set up a meeting with my friends. We need to hear what you have to offer."

On that street corner in New York City, our new life was born. We've been leading workshops ever since, doing our best to articulate how we are living in a way that others can catch it for themselves. Like Bankei, we realize that all of the workshops and pain and striving was necessary for us because it's what we did, but it wasn't what caused our enlightenment. ***We've discovered that transformation is not an achievement but rather a lifestyle where you're actively being a Yes to how your life is unfolding, moment-by-moment.*** And it's happening far more easily for others these days than it originally did for us.

WHEN YOU'RE LOOKING, DOORS OPEN

If you're reading this book, then you're looking for something. It may be as simple as wanting to be able to experience all of the "small" moments of your life. It may be that some larger event has catapulted you into a journey where you're reevaluating your life and life circumstances. You may be interested in mining all the possibilities available to you so that you and your family can have a rich and fulfilling life. Or maybe, like our friend Menna, who wrote the Foreword for this book, you secretly think that you're broken or at the very least, mildly messed up. Whatever your starting point, if you're willing to fully engage in this moment without judging yourself or others for what you see, then the possibility of Instantaneous Transformation and enlightenment will become available to you.

2

BEING A YES TO LIFE

*W*hen you are operating as though what happens in your life is supposed to happen, then life becomes an adventure. When life is a discovery, an ever-expanding experience of living, when every occurrence is held as though it is perfect, you are enlightened. When you are a genuine Yes to how life is showing up, when you interact with the people that you meet as though you are meant to be there with them, then this moment is your destiny and life becomes a joy.

We've all been raised in forward-thinking cultures where we learned that something in the future will produce a sense of well-being or "OKness" which we then strive to achieve. It is this very striving, we've discovered, that produces dissatisfaction. The constant need to achieve what we think is better than what we have in the current moment stresses us and places us in an endless cycle of pain. *We've been taught that when we achieve certain goals, we'll be happy and satisfied. But it's not true. Happiness is not determined by circumstance and neither is well-being.*

Instantaneous Transformation happens when you're living in the current moment of your life. This moment right now is all there is. Something in the future will not get here until it does, and when it does, it will occur as a moment of now.

Anything that you disagree with is what you're stuck with. But what you allow to be the way it is allows you the freedom to be yourself. This moment is perfect exactly as it is and in fact cannot be different than it is/was.

The moment we stopped working on ourselves to get "better," our lives instantaneously transformed. This has profoundly impacted everything. What we have learned is not to take ourselves so seriously and not to work so hard to get somewhere. We have learned that life shows up exactly as it does in each moment, and it rarely, if ever, shows up to meet our preferences. *If meeting your preferences determines your well-being, chances are you'll never feel well, even if you meet your goals.*

IT IS WHAT IT IS!

We often hear people say, "Oh, OK, I accept this situation. It is what it is." Roughly translated, that means, "I don't like it...but I'll get over it." This kind of acceptance is No in disguise. When you are a No to your life, even a disguised No, then your well-being or lack thereof is blamed on circumstances. You can either be the victim of your life or the author of your life. As the victim of your life, circumstances determine your sense of well-being, satisfaction and accomplishment. If it doesn't work out, it's always caused from outside you. What we're talking about is truly being a Yes to the way your life is unfolding in each moment.

Your life shows up as a reflection of how you're being. All is unfolding exactly as it is intended to. When you disagree with the way your life is showing up, which by the way is how we have all been taught to relate to life, then you are in a constant state of incompletion and disharmony. If you're resisting the way your life is showing up and saying No, you perpetuate those very things you resist. Being a Yes to your life and the way your life is showing up in each moment shifts your reality and allows you to truly take control of your own life. Saying Yes and meaning it is a skill set. With practice, you'll get better at being a Yes, regardless of the circumstances.

PRACTICAL ENLIGHTENMENT INCLUDES THE ABILITY TO TRANSCEND YOUR BRATTY NATURE

As children, we discover our independence in reaction to and in opposition to the wishes of our parents or other people in authority. This disagreement with what our life requests of us goes forward in time and, if not observed objectively, will continue from birth to death. The result will be a life devoid of well-being and satisfaction. You may in fact acquire great wealth or personal power but it will not be enough to quench your thirst for well-being and self-expression.

Well-being and feeling satisfied come from being congruent with your life as it shows up in each moment. Satisfaction is not available when you subscribe to the idea that something, someday is going to come along that will save you from your current circumstances. If, however, you discover the knack of being a Yes to whatever your life requests of you, life will be fulfilling and satisfying.

The secret to happiness and well-being is interacting with your life as though your life is your idea. But we've all been raised in the paradigm of No, the paradigm of complaint where whatever is happening in our lives is not enough, where someday, someone or something will save us from ourselves and provide well-being. This forward-thinking way of life is the source of all dissatisfaction. We live in a sea of disagreement where the agreed-upon reality is one of complaint – that this moment is not enough, that we need something more, different or better to complete us. As long as you view life through this paradigm or system of seeing, there will never be well-being.

We once traveled through London's Heathrow airport as we were heading home from leading a seminar in Cambridge. There we encountered a young lady who was checking tickets and processing luggage. We asked her, "Are you having a good day?"

Her response was, "Not really, but it will get better when I leave here."

The problem is that wherever she is isn't "it" and isn't enough. From that perspective you continuously look forward to something that will save you from the boredom of your life. Enlightenment involves choosing to have what you have in your life in the current moment. In other words, being a Yes to how your life is showing up, as opposed to resisting or wishing it was different – complaining to yourself that life is not fair. Our cultural training holds that striving to achieve something "better," as laudable while just allowing your life to be as it is, as lazy. This training says it is "right" to set goals for yourself based on cultural mores and beliefs and then you must achieve those goals. Most of the planet adheres to this paradigm.

But that is not the paradigm for well-being and satisfaction. Being kind to yourself is, saying Yes to the way your life is unfolding in each moment is. Please understand that we're not advocating complacency or settling in your life. We are not saying that having goals is "bad" and that passionately pursuing your dreams is wrong. What we are talking about is this moment and Being Here for it, right where you are, experiencing your life directly, rather than thinking about how to live your life "right." ***This moment is the springboard into your greatness, creativity, well-being and self-expression.***

3

ACHIEVING YOUR GOALS AND BEING IN THE MOMENT

*A*gain, we're not implying that you shouldn't have goals. What we are saying is that there is a different way to go about fulfilling your heartfelt desires, where there is well-being every step of the way and where you recognize that the result is not more important than this moment. Here is an example:

Our friend Menna sold her first novel, *Men, Money and Chocolate*, to a publisher that liked it so much that they also paid her an advance for a sequel, which she had yet to write. Thrilled, Menna wrote her second novel and submitted it to them. They rejected it. Feeling stressed but determined, she wrote another version of a sequel and the publisher didn't like it either. Discouraged, she closed herself off from her husband and her world while she got down to business. After much stress and struggle she completed yet an entirely different novel, which she submitted. They rejected that attempt also.

By now Menna was tired, irritable, and feeling like perhaps her first book was an accident. *Maybe it was just a fluke that I wrote something good in the first place,* she thought. Sitting at her desk, she would gaze longingly at the garden out back, wishing to be out in nature; but thinking that this was off-purpose, she would wrestle her attention back to her project.

Menna eventually wrote an outline for yet another novel, which she submitted to her publisher. As a result, they called her in for a meeting and told her she needed to go in another direction. How she was going to go about it, they didn't know. But if something didn't happen soon, she would be obligated to give back her advance.

Tired, frustrated, confused, upset and feeling pressured to get it done – in truth it was time to take a break. Fortunately for her, Menna was registered to attend one of our transformational immersion courses in Costa Rica along with her husband Artur. Once there, she let everything go. She forgot about home, forgot about being a writer, let go of trying to get somewhere and trying to get her book done. She simply invested herself in being where she was while being there for the experience. She rode horses, zipped through the tree tops on a canopy tour, ate delicious food, enjoyed friends and made new ones. She also sat in the course room and truly listened.

Menna marveled at the birds, how the rain could fall hard enough to practically drown out speech, only to have the sky clear a short time later, and she watched the ground steam as the sun reemerged. She discovered her husband once again. She enjoyed Artur – really enjoyed him. She fully engaged. She slowed down. She fell into the moment and as a byproduct effortlessly bypassed her intelligence and accessed her genius.

It was when Menna returned home to Cambridge, England, that she actually remembered she had a project that was due. She had literally forgotten all about it. *Oh yes*, she said to herself, *I have a book to write.* Three weeks later it was complete. *Happier Than She's Ever Been* was a great success. Each book she has written since has been easier and more successful than the one that came before.

When you push yourself to get somewhere, common wisdom says that you will accomplish great things. But what if stressing yourself to get to where you think you need to be is not a necessary component to being successful? There is only one of you on a planet of billions of people. You already are a success.

PLANNING AND THE MOMENT

You may be confused as to how to be in the moment and still make plans for the future. It's simple. If you are sitting at your desk, for instance, making hotel reservations for a family vacation you want to take, then that is your moment. Planning is what your moment includes. There is a distinct difference between daydreaming about how much better things will be once you go on vacation and actually taking the steps to set up a trip.

We travel regularly to give seminars in foreign countries so we have to make airline, car, hotel and facility reservations far in advance. When we are planning the trip, that's what we are doing. We are not, however, thinking our lives will improve once we get to where we are going. We also have come to recognize that there is a natural rhythm to completing projects, which extends to making plans. If setting something up becomes "difficult," then it is highly likely that we are forcing things somehow.

PRACTICAL ENLIGHTENMENT INVOLVES EMBRACING PARADOX

It has been said that the doors to enlightenment are guarded by two lions – one that represents confusion, the other paradox. A paradox is when two seemingly opposing ideas are, in fact, both true. The classic example is the saying, "Water, water everywhere and not a drop to drink." This statement seems confusing and conflicting yet paradoxically, if you are floating on a raft in the middle of the ocean, there is water as far as the eye can see, but there will be no drinkable water in sight.

When you are in the moment, there is nothing that needs to be done, and often there are things to do. For example, this moment is perfect. It needs nothing to be complete. Yet if you want to eat on clean dishes, you will need to wash them after they have been used. If you have said something unkind to someone, you don't need to apologize in order to be a "perfect" you, yet if you don't there are likely to be consequences, such as losing a friend or even a marriage.

Enlightenment is not for or against anything. Goals are about going for something in the future. Can you experience enlightenment and still have goals? Of course you can. Yet if your goals become more important than this moment, you are truly lost.

Transformation is Instantaneous. It happens in a moment. However, transformation and the experience of enlightenment are also cumulative. The more you invest in being present, the deeper the experience becomes. And while you can't authentically "be present" in order to produce positive results, you will find that as a byproduct of being present you are naturally more productive, effective and satisfied.

4

PRACTICAL ENLIGHTENMENT
INVOLVES COMPLETION

S ome people believe in Karma, where people come back lifetime after lifetime until they complete those things that have been left unfinished in the past. The cycle of rebirth is all about completion. Anything that is incomplete comes around again.

People go through their lives avoiding what they do not prefer to do and so those things stay incomplete. And the universe is based in a cycle of birth, continuance and death – or beginning, middle and end. The universe keeps moving toward completion and everything that is left incomplete keeps coming back.

Transformation happens as you discover how to be a Yes to everything your life requests of you so that you keep completing those requests. This frees you from your past because you are not holding onto and bringing back that which is incomplete. It really is about living non-preferentially, where you do what life requests of you, and you do it as though it was your idea in the first place. It is about surrendering to the moment. If you go about things with resistance then there is leftover residue. What you resist or don't want to do keeps coming around to be completed. And life keeps showing up as it does in each current moment of now. If you are a Yes to how your life is showing up that moment is complete. Having run its full course it is finished.

Here is an example. Let's say it is night, you have eaten dinner and you don't want to do the dishes, so you set them in the sink. They are there when you wake up in the morning. And, if you really resisted doing them and you didn't initially rinse them, everything is stuck on the dish. So now, they are still in need of cleaning but it is more difficult than if you had just taken a moment to complete them the night before. Avoiding the dishes and wishing they weren't in your sink doesn't wash them.

Again, with Practical Enlightenment you are not trying to "get over" your life or get to somewhere better. You are simply here, living your life. It has to do with how you deal with the ordinary, day-to-day requests that life makes. It's about operating as if what you're doing is your idea, whatever that may be, not something that comes in from the outside. Most of us, however, are acculturated to complain about circumstances that we don't like or didn't plan even though those complaints will not change the situation. Complaining – saying No – will not only add agitation to the situation but will also do nothing to resolve it. When you say Yes and mean it, however, life becomes a magical adventure – even when you are in a crowded airport and have just found out that your flight has been cancelled.

I LOVE AIRPORTS!

People were surprised when Kat stood up at one of our seminars and without preamble, enthusiastically announced, "I love airports!" It was a Monday evening in early spring and we had encouraged people to come up to the front of the room and talk about what was happening in their lives. Kat is a petite, dynamic woman in her late twenties, with shoulder length auburn hair. Standing on the balls of her feet and leaning toward the group, she grinned as she said, "Recently I flew back from the West Coast and I had a layover in Chicago where they'd had a sudden snow storm. When my flight arrived, they announced that my connecting flight was cancelled and they directed us to a white courtesy phone. I picked up the receiver and was connected to a perfectly nice woman who helped me re-book my flight. Then I went to a restaurant where I had a perfectly nice meal. And I got to walk around and people-watch and visit the airport shops. I was amazed that I had no complaints. I have transformation to thank for that. I used to be so upset and any little unexpected change would make me mad. At least that was how I thought of it at the time."

"What do you mean?" Ariel asked.

"Well," Kat said, "I used to actually think that someone or something could make me mad."

"Ahh, yes," Shya said. "Most people blame outside circumstances when their anger or annoyance is triggered.

"We've been programmed by the cultures we have been raised in to believe that our upsets are caused by events or other people rather than realizing that our upsets are vestiges of our own un-experienced emotions. So when you blame the circumstances as though they are the cause of your emotions you are not being honest that the emotions are generated from within yourself and so they don't complete themselves. They are not truly experienced. Their cause is placed outside you, as if you have no control over them and, in fact, initially you don't. Initially your emotional experience is a stimulus/ response, re-stimulation mechanism. As we said before, this is part of the cultural heritage, or agreed-upon belief that the culture holds as a truth."

"And anything you resist, or don't fully experience, persists, and grows stronger, eventually dominating your life," Ariel continued. "This is why many people have anger and annoyance on tap. They mistakenly think that someone or something *caused* their upset. But what they don't realize is that they are pre-charged and any disturbance can set off an explosion. It's similar to a gun. It is reasonable to expect that if you pull the trigger on a loaded gun the gun will fire. But if there is no gunpowder in the cartridge then no matter how many times you pull the trigger there won't be any resulting 'bang.' The better you get at saying Yes to what is happening, the less likely you are to have flare-ups when life doesn't go the way you want."

"In general people rarely allow themselves to feel what they are feeling," Shya said. "They are habituated to blaming their emotions on something outside themselves so those feelings can never complete. What it takes is to feel what you are feeling, not resist it, and not blame it on something outside yourself. The act of allowing those body sensations and thoughts to run without associating them or attaching them to anything else will allow them to complete themselves – i.e. be experienced out.

"Life is unfolding perfectly in each moment so you haven't done it wrong, even if you have blamed circumstances for your emotions. But when you do, these emotions keep coming back to be completed. What it takes is compassion for yourself and others. It also takes letting go of blame/being right that someone else is responsible for your experience. You need to let go of your story that your parents are to blame, that your life is to blame, even that you are to blame. It is simply about being with your experience and feeling what you are feeling without judging yourself."

"Exactly!" Kat said with a grin. "Now it takes a lot before I lose my center. And you know what's cool?" she asked the room at large. "I didn't have to *tell* myself not to be annoyed – I just wasn't.

"I've heard the two of you say over the years that 'nothing matters and everything matters' – that nothing is worth losing your state over and it's possible to go about your life as if everything you do and every moment is important, not just the moments I would prefer. I realize that for me, it's no longer just an idea. I actually go about my life this way. Of course I lose it from time to time and I get annoyed but it's become so much easier to see my annoyance and not judge myself for it."

"That's brilliant, Kat," Shya said. "Most people spend a lot of time in transit – in airports, morning commutes, in line at the bank or supermarket, and they think that in those moments their lives are on pause while they're traveling to their intended destination or until they step up to the window to do their business. While waiting to get where they are going, people complain and even socialize via complaints. The miracle of air travel, the wonder of a car, are both deemed ordinary. But when you're here and say Yes to what is happening in this moment of your life, then even 'ordinary' moments, mundane tasks and events are extraordinary."

Kat grinned again. "I love my life!" she declared and without further ado, she returned to her seat.

Clearly Kat has learned a valuable skill set – the ability to say Yes to situations over which she apparently has no control. She has discovered how to treat the circumstances as if they were her preference and as though they are her idea to begin with which gives her ultimate control. All it takes is wholeheartedly engaging with life as it unfolds.

This ability to say Yes to what is happening in your life gets a little more complicated when it seems as if you have a choice and as if you could choose incorrectly. In the following example, as told by Ariel, she relates a story of apparently surrendering to Shya. In truth, it is a sophisticated version of being a Yes to her life and life choices.

ARIEL AT A CROSSROADS

Shya and I were driving into New York City to begin one of our Transformational weekend seminars. As is our practice, we allowed ourselves plenty of travel time in case the traffic was heavy. But on this particular day there was an accident on the road that made the trip significantly longer than usual.

Originally we had intended to drive by the hotel, check in, then continue to the workshop location, park the car near the venue and have a quick dinner before the course. But as we were driving into the Lincoln Tunnel, which runs under the Hudson River between New Jersey and New York, it was much later than we had anticipated and time to reevaluate our plans.

Shya was of the opinion that we could get it all done. I thought it was safer to skip the hotel and check in after the evening session. The only problem with my idea was that when we had checked in late in the past, often the only rooms left were the noisy ones by the ice machine or the elevator. There had even been an instance when the hotel had overbooked and had absolutely no rooms left when we arrived. They'd sent us to a different hotel, which made for a very late evening.

Even so, I was concerned about the traffic. Going across town in Manhattan on a Friday evening can sometimes be a very slow process. We knew this from experience. I thought it safest to go directly to the parking lot near the course. In fact, I was fairly sure that would be the best way to go. As we approached the end of the tunnel, we reached a crossroads – literally and figuratively. If we went to the seminar venue, we needed to turn right. If we went to the hotel first, we needed to turn left. My vote was to go downtown to the seminar when Shya said to me again, "Ariel, we can get it all done. Let's go by the hotel."

"OK," I said.

In that moment I realized I was at my own personal crossroads, too. It would have been easy to go along with Shya's plan but quietly, privately, secretly hold onto my own idea. I recognized as we made the left to head to the hotel, it would be almost natural to watch for Shya's plan to fail. I could easily have surreptitiously looked to be right. If we turned down a block that had a traffic backup or if we missed a light and had to sit for an extra moment or two at a red light, my original idea would have proved to be the superior one. If I didn't truly surrender to Shya's point of view, I would mentally be rooting for a delay in order to prove that my perspective was right after all. Shya would have to lose in order for me to win. But I would lose also since we'd have to be late for our seminar in order for me to be right. Instead, I turned the "alive" way – going in the direction our car was traveling rather than mentally being against it. If for some unforeseen reason we didn't have time for dinner before work, it would have been my plan, my choice, and I wouldn't be victimized by the circumstances.

As I surrendered to going to the hotel first as though it was my idea, I intended this to be an excellent choice and I noticed how a sense of calm settled in. I was able to enjoy the ride. I placed a hand on Shya's leg and felt his warmth through the fabric of his pants. I watched people hurrying to their destinations. I could see lane openings ahead on my side of the car that couldn't be seen from the driver's seat and I acted as a co-pilot, partnering Shya in getting to our destination. I felt my shoulders and face relax. I was instantaneously in sync with Shya, the traffic, my environment and of course, my life.

It was a simple event, yet profound. I could see how in the basic enculturation process, we're taught to either fight or give in, but rarely to partner. Both fighting and giving in are about being right. If I didn't wholeheartedly choose to do what I was actually doing, like going to the hotel first, then I would be a victim of my life in general and of Shya in particular.

Shya and I are practiced at surrendering to each other. When one of us has a strong opinion for or against something, the other generally defers as if we were the originator of the action, not the follower. And even though this has been our style of operating for many years, I had never before so clearly seen the choice, the crossroads, where one road led to tension and separation and the other led to intimacy.

Shya was accurate, by the way. Maybe it's more true to say that we were accurate. We had enough time to go to the hotel first and get it all done. We checked in, got a lovely room, drove downtown, enjoyed a bite to eat and arrived at the seminar relaxed and refreshed. And you know what? If we had guessed incorrectly and hadn't had time for dinner, we would have enjoyed getting hungry and having our meal later.

Along the same lines, if you wash the dishes as though that act is important and you would prefer to do nothing else in that moment, then magically, it becomes a satisfying, fulfilling experience. If you go about your life being a Yes, as if everything you do is your idea rather than something put upon you, life becomes fulfilling and satisfying. Actually it doesn't become – it is.

LISTENING YOUR WAY
TO ENLIGHTENMENT

One of the most valuable skills a person can learn is how to listen. You may think you already know how to listen but your ability to listen and truly hear what another person is saying from his or her perspective is not a static, set-in-place thing. It varies from moment to moment and is impacted by a wide variety of influences. It's important to bring your awareness to how you listen or don't listen, without judging what you see.

Our definition of awareness is: A nonjudgmental, non-preferential seeing. It's an objective, noncritical witnessing of the nature or what we call the "isness" of any particular circumstance or situation. It can be described as an ongoing process in which you are bringing yourself back to the moment, rather than complaining silently about how you would prefer this moment to be.

When you listen with awareness, you will discover many things, such as:

Anything you resist hearing, you get stuck with.

Surprisingly, some of the things people get stuck with are "good" things. Have you ever found it hard to take a compliment? If someone praises you, do you find it hard to hear? Do you ever walk away from the interaction rebutting the comment in your thoughts?

With awareness, you'll discover that your ability to hear is affected by many things, such as the amount of sleep you're getting, whether or not you're hungry, if you feel "on the spot," if you are trying to get somewhere (get something done) or if you have the idea that you are "no good" at something. Your ability to listen can be impacted by an infinite number of factors which is why slapping a label on yourself like, "I'm a good listener" or "I'm a bad listener" is inaccurate and it precludes you from being present to see how you're currently interacting with your life.

In the case of this book, reading is akin to listening. You're listening to what we have to say via the conduit of reading the written word. Most people, however, feel compelled to do something extra with what is being said. This is an automatic response of the mind. In a nanosecond, after you "hear" what is being said, you compare it to what you already know. Then, based on past information or experiences in your mental database, you automatically agree or disagree with what is being said. You flip through your mental file folder of notes about the subject being discussed and compare it to things you've already read or heard. Suddenly the moment is no longer fresh or new or alive. Instead you think, it's "just like...."

THE GRANOLA TREE

"Mama, I saw a granola tree today!" our grandson Max announced with excitement. "A granola tree?" our daughter Diana asked him. Then she remembered that the week before, when she and Max were walking in Brooklyn, she had pointed out a magnolia tree. The flowers on a magnolia tree bloom early in a fleshy pink and white and the leaves fill in later, making the tree tall, stately, and gloriously blossomed with its branches reaching to the sky. The word "magnolia" was a new one for Max but he was very familiar with "granola." He'd often eaten it for breakfast and Diana made it from scratch. So when he saw the magnolia tree, his mind reached for what he recalled. This made sense according to a child's logic, and although it wasn't completely accurate, it was at least a reasonable facsimile.

As we grow, our minds may get more sophisticated than young Max's, but they still work in a similar manner. They take what we know and use it as a substitute for something new. And like a granola tree, the result can be equally inaccurate. Also, most of us are regularly experiencing a glut of input. Have you ever been on the phone with your email open in front of you and maybe there's a television show going in the background? Do you find yourself listening with half an ear? Do you ever fill in the gaps with what you expect to hear or want to hear or with a word that fits your prior agenda or perspective? Has it ever occurred to you just how much your ability to listen and really hear affects virtually all areas of your life?

LISTENING AND ITS EFFECT ON LEARNING

Andrew Gideon and his wife Amy have a website company, TAG Online, where they design, implement and host websites. Although Andy has his Master's degree in Computer Science, when he attended one of our first business courses, he was surprised to discover that despite all of his years of education, he'd never stopped to consider the act of listening and its effect on the learning process. Over the course of that weekend, we were all focused on listening to each other as we explored the impediments to True Listening. Andy subsequently wrote an article about his experience and is gracious enough to let us reprint it here:

If you're reading this, you've probably spent more time in a classroom than you can remember. It's likely that you continue to spend time in similar settings, maybe conferences, meetings, sales presentations, or the like. You've spent a lifetime listening to teachers, speakers, reading books and materials, and watching presentations, all in the quest for information. But do you really know what you're doing?

We have a name for this: Learning. But do you really know an effective way to learn? Have you ever even considered the questions, "How well can I learn?" and "How can I learn better?" Despite the thousands of hours that many of us have invested in learning situations, we've really never learned how to learn. It was always something that we just sort of figured out on the fly.

There is an existing technology that can make a dramatic difference in how you learn. It isn't a study method, a memory aid, or a way to read faster. The major component of this technology has a deceptively simple name and you probably think it's something you already do. It's called "listening." But don't let the name fool you. When you think you're listening, you may be doing something completely different. I've learned that what I used to call "listening" is not what I mean when I use the word now.

I recently attended a business workshop given by Ariel and Shya Kane, entitled *Transformation in the Workplace*. As part of the seminar, we explored what it means to truly listen, to intentionally hear what is being said from the point of view of the person who is speaking. How many times do you remember sitting in a presentation or a class, engaging in a casual conversation and hearing something that gave you an idea? It happens to me a lot. I follow the thoughts to see what the new information might mean, or how I might use it. But by the time my attention returns to the speaker, I'm totally lost.

If the speaker says something that sounds like what I've previously learned, I think "I know that" to myself. Since I already know – or believe that I do – I don't bother to really listen and hear it. And then there's no chance for me to see that what the speaker is saying is new or different. Even if I *did* happen to know the facts involved, the speaker's perspective is different from my own. If I truly listen, I can acquire a new insight into things. When I think, "I already know that," it closes me off from hearing the truth and therefore learning. And if you hear yourself saying, "I agree" or "I disagree," you are converting someone else's words into something you already know. Again, you're stopping yourself from truly hearing.

Having an agenda is another hindrance to listening. Consider a sales presentation for a product that I've already decided I want. I'm probably listening through my agenda, storing information to make the case that the product should be purchased. At the same time, though, I'm filtering out any information that might serve to change my mind – or at least cause me to further question my purchase. Because all information is passing through the filter of my agenda, I'm not truly listening to the speaker, and I've lost the opportunity to learn. This filtering process works exactly the same way when my agenda is to not purchase the product.

I also discovered that if I'm practicing what I'm about to say while someone else is speaking, I'm not listening. This is especially true when I'm about to give a planned presentation. I generally don't remember who spoke before me, much less what they said during their talk because I was busy practicing my talk in my mind.

One final hindrance I want to mention is "feeling badly" for not listening. Punishing yourself is just one more way to avoid listening and learning, and it doesn't accomplish anything positive. When you notice that you're not listening, you have a choice. You can feel badly, or you can move your attention away from yourself and back onto the speaker. By choosing wisely, you are placing yourself back into a state where you're listening and learning.

Since attending the Kanes' course, I have discovered that listening goes far beyond just learning. It is about truly hearing what is being said, whether it's coming from a teacher, a coworker, a supervisor, or a client. The simple act of truly listening allows a dramatic shift, a transformation in what you can accomplish in your life. I urge you to try it for yourself. Then, when someone tells you how you've suddenly become much more effective, productive and easy to be with, you'll really be able to hear it.

I KNOW THAT! OR DO I?

"Can you afford the arrogance to think that there is nothing that you don't know, the knowing of which would transform your life?" – Werner Erhard

Looking for similarities or differences is something the mind is geared to do, and if you hear something that challenges your beliefs, you can easily dismiss it. At Dartmouth College in Hanover, New Hampshire, a study proved that a part of the brain fires up to dismiss or block new or inconvenient information that will conflict with your current beliefs. ***For example, if you believe that life is difficult, you're likely to dismiss anything that suggests otherwise.***

Another inhibitor to engaging in life directly happens when you are worried about looking good or feeling stupid. This leads to the "I know that" syndrome, where the need to be right and the desire to not be considered stupid superimposes the idea, "I know that already." This makes it impossible to experience life directly because you believe an internal conversation that says, "I know that," which inhibits your ability to look and see the truth of something.

"I know that" is a stage that kids go through when they're trying to be adults or trying to fit in. One time, we were on vacation in Cape Cod, when our granddaughter Hanna was ten years old and was sitting in the back of our car. We were taking her and her father to the bus station to catch a bus that would take them to the airport. We'd never been to that particular drop-off point before and we were trying to find it. The conversation went like this:

Shya: I don't know where the terminal is.

Hanna: I do!

Then, without missing a beat, she added: What's a "terminal?"

Not only did Hanna not know where the bus station was, she didn't even know the meaning of the word "terminal." But clearly she had already learned the "I know that" stance that most of us learn and then sophisticate over time.

There is a vast difference between already knowing everything and being here to experience your life. Your mind is a closed system. When you "know," you don't really see. When you "know," your knowledge precedes you and acts as a set of blinders so that you don't actually experience being where you are. Rather, you live through a template of past knowledge, events and/or beliefs.

As you invest yourself in being here in this moment of now, life and your senses become richer and you have the capacity to experience things anew and to see things you have never seen before. As you keep investing in this moment of now, serenity, well-being, feeling OK being you, feeling good in your own skin, not having to second-guess your choices and trusting that you will do the right thing will all become as natural to you as breathing. And you will be here to experience all that life has to offer along the way.

If you believe you already know something, you'll argue for that as the only truth and you won't have the ability or the space to see any other possibility.

THE WINDSHIELD-WIPER EFFECT

Our minds are skilled at diverting what is being said in favor of what we already know. In this way, we disregard anything that is inconsistent or inconvenient according to our already held beliefs, casting aside new information so it never really gets in.

You may have heard the phrase, "The scientist affects the experiment." In other words, what you're expecting colors your perception. It's as if the mind sweeps away inconvenient information like a windshield wiper whisks away rain that falls on a car's windshield.

When our first book, *Working on Yourself Doesn't Work,* was published, a woman wrote a scathing review of it on a book website stating: "Suggesting that your problems can transform in an instant is highly irresponsible. Everybody knows that it takes years of therapy and drugs."

"Common sense is the collection of prejudices acquired by age eighteen." – Albert Einstein

We tend to hold certain beliefs so sacred that giving them up would cause us to question the underpinnings of our lives. So we settle for being comfortably uncomfortable and being in perpetual rolling upsets rather than face the unknown.

Your beliefs began in the culture where you grew up, from your family, your community and from the schools you attended. In order to hear anything in a fresh manner, you have to hold in abeyance your mind's propensity to compare, to add information, to agree or disagree. Most of all, you need to let go of your point of view, including what you want to say when the speaker has finished talking.

"The bird fights its way out of the egg. The egg is the world. Who would be born must first destroy a world."

The above quote from Hermann Hesse's *Demian* refers to the fact that the chick must destroy the egg in order to come into being. In the same way, you have to be willing to let go of what you know and hold as true in order to experience the moment. When Einstein initially postulated his theory of relativity prior to the advent of quantum physics, people called it *gobbledygook*. They couldn't understand it because it was outside their current paradigm or system of seeing.

And so, in order to hear something in a new way, you must stop comparing what is being said to what you already know. At first it seems impossible to suspend random thought in order to listen with a receptive, open, available mind. It takes a bit of practice to give up your point of view and your need to be right, in order to allow in something new. But as you keep engaging in what is actually happening in your life rather than talking to yourself about your preferences, you are stimulating and growing new neural pathways while you stop running over old well-worn tracks in your mind.

LISTENING IS A CATALYST FOR INSTANTANEOUS TRANSFORMATION

When you are truly in the moment, your life transforms – in an instant. It doesn't take time and it isn't a one-time event. As you get more skilled at being present, transformation becomes a lifestyle. It's not a goal. It happens as a by-product of being here, in this moment, right now, rather than being caught in the forward momentum of trying to get somewhere, even if it's as simple as getting to work in the morning without being "hassled."

In the next section, we meet a young woman named Val who found a spontaneous and unanticipated resolution to a long-standing problem, simply through listening. Her story, told from her own point of view, demonstrates that when you step into the moment, whatever you've been putting up with will simply resolve itself. You don't have to create a plan to facilitate a resolution. Some "problems" have become so normal you may have resigned yourself to the idea that they are simply parts of life. But when you are a Yes to your life, your ability to be present and appropriate comes to the foreground and often creates unexpected and miraculous outcomes.

WHEN "HEY MOMMY" TURNS INTO "GOOD MORNING!"

At 23, Val was thrilled to have gotten her first job after college, working for a PR firm in New York City. The job allowed her to utilize her schooling, communication skills and even her knowledge of the French language. But when she tried to imagine the types of challenges she would face in her new job, she never imagined that walking that last half block to the building where she worked would be the most daunting.

As an Amer-Asian (her dad is of Korean descent, her mom, Caucasian), Val has lustrous deep brown hair, a compact and shapely figure and an elegant air about her. In the beginning, her job was typically fast-paced with a significant learning curve as she got to know the clients and juggled the tasks that were hers to manage – phones, emails, packages and deadlines. But as she slipped into the routine of a busy office, she was excited about the work and her newly minted career. All of this was about to change one sultry summer morning in an unexpected way.

Val bounded up the stairs of the PATH train that takes riders from New Jersey to their Manhattan jobs each day. When she exited the station at 23rd Street and 6th Avenue, it was already very warm outside; the concrete buildings all around her were still holding warmth from the previous day. There was the slightest rancid smell of garbage in the air but oddly enough, she liked it. It smelled like New York City in the summer – big and hot and bustling with people. Like a girl in love, she was thoroughly excited to be there and part of it all.

In a loose, easy stride, Val sauntered toward 28th Street, happy that she was wearing strappy little flats and that she didn't need to wear stockings beneath her flirty skirt. As the sun peeked out from between the tall buildings, she took a deep breath and felt on top of the world. As she turned the corner leaving 6th Avenue behind her, 28th Street was alive and bustling. That particular block was the heart of the flower district and in the stores that lined the street were flowers of all types, year-round. One storefront specialized in dried arrangements while the next had orchids. Others had towering green leafy plants and still others had boxes of cut flowers such as roses or tropical Hawaiian blooms. No matter the weather, this block always looked and smelled fresh in the mornings. It was where flower shop owners and designers flocked to buy their fresh flowers, ribbons, baskets and all that went into floral designs.

When Val was about halfway between the corner and her building, she saw a man leaning on a doorframe, who began to give her a catcall. He made her skin crawl and her bright outlook on the day got dim. "Hey Mommy. Mmmm you're looking *gooooood*," he said, drawing out his words. "You look good enough to eat."

Val hunched her shoulders and kept on moving. Just looking at him made her want to run home and take a shower. *What a creep*, she thought, as his long, low whistle of appreciation followed her up the street. With relief, she finally stepped into the vestibule of the building where she worked, glad that this small ordeal was over. Little did she know it had just begun.

For months, this man hassled her on her way to work whenever he was out front – which was often. She tried approaching her building on the opposite side of the street but he usually caught sight of her coming and his cat calls and whistles got louder to make up for the distance. Mornings became a tense time during which Val felt as if she had to run a gauntlet each day in order to get to work. While she still loved her job, these daily interactions dimmed her enthusiasm because she started her workday worried, not knowing which days it would be "safe" to walk down the street and which ones that man would make the short walk a living nightmare.

It was an early spring weekend when all of that changed, but she didn't know it at the time. Val's bosses invited her to attend a seminar that was being offered by Ariel and Shya Kane, who were their business coaches, about Money, Success and Happiness. It was called *Wealth as a Lifestyle*, which sounded good to her and they said it was about *Instantaneous Transformation* – whatever that meant.

That Friday before heading down to the workshop, Val stayed at work a bit later than usual. Feeling a little nervous about attending a self-help course with her bosses, she lingered in the bathroom, fussing with her hair and makeup. When she looked in the mirror, Val saw her own dark eyes gazing back looking all serious and subdued. She snorted and cracked a smile at herself. *What might her bosses see*, she reasoned, *that was so terrible?*

Later that evening when she arrived at the seminar, the Kanes greeted her warmly. Val felt herself relax a little but she wished she could go back uptown to her desk and bury herself in work because that would be easier than being with people as they arrived, most of whom were strangers to her. She had planned to sit unobtrusively in the back but another young woman, Christina, had invited Val to sit next to her, so she sat much closer to the front than she had envisioned.

At first Ariel and Shya introduced the idea of listening – truly listening to hear what another has to say from his or her perspective. They encouraged people to let go of their agendas and what had happened during the day and to use listening as a tool to get into the moment.

"When you get into the moment, your life will transform," Shya promised.

Intrigued with the idea, she leaned forward slightly in her seat. There had been plenty of times during that day when she had worried about the future, mentally chewing on things she was afraid to start for fear of getting it all wrong. Maybe there was something to this listening thing.

Next came the Three Principles of Instantaneous Transformation. Val quickly lost track of who was saying what since the Kanes had this way of speaking in which one would start a sentence and the other would finish it. Neither one of them looked bothered by the other or seemed to feel like they were being interrupted. It was almost as if they were operating on the same wavelength or reading the same script, although it was obvious that their words were spontaneous and unscripted.

"The First Principle of Instantaneous Transformation is: Anything you resist persists and grows stronger and dominates your life," they said. "Take a look at your own life and see if there is anything or anyone you've been resisting. Hasn't that person or situation been something that you think about more and more?"

Boy, you could say that again! Val thought. Immediately her mind had flashed on her stalker – that creepy guy who just wouldn't leave her alone. For a moment her mind wandered. She started to think about how grateful she was that she left her job each day after he was gone so that she only had to avoid him in the mornings. Of course there was the occasional lunch hour as well where she couldn't easily walk in his direction.

Suddenly Val realized that the Kanes had continued speaking; the evening had moved on but she hadn't been there for it. A blush of crimson spread across her face and she surreptitiously glanced at her bosses sitting down the row on her right to see if they had noticed. Nope. They were listening. She hastily started listening again herself as she realized that she hadn't been "gone" for that long after all.

"The Second Principle of Instantaneous Transformation is this: No two things can occupy the same space at the same time. In other words no one but you can possibly be sitting in your chair in this particular moment."

Shya then gave a fellow on the end of the row a challenge, "Be different than you are right now," he said as he snapped his fingers. "Too late! Now has gone by!" The man grinned.

"How about *now*?" Shya said as he snapped his fingers, "Too late! Now has gone by. Your life shows up moment-by-moment and in that moment it can only be the way that it is because it is. If you see this, then there is no need for blame or shame or regret. Your life is unfolding perfectly right now."

Val found herself a little confused by this. Sometimes some things didn't feel perfect to her.

As if reading her mind Ariel continued, "If things don't feel perfect to you, then chances are there is something that you're resisting or complaining about, something you're judging, saying 'No' to or you're wishing it could

be different. But we've already established that what
you resist persists and grows stronger," she added with
a smile. "It's a law of physics – for every action there
is an equal and opposite reaction. The more you resist
something the more you keep it in place."

"This brings us to the Third Principle of Instantaneous
Transformation," Shya segued. "This is the 'awareness'
principle. Our definition of awareness is a nonjudgmental
seeing or observation of things. The Third Principle is:
Anything you see without judging it completes itself. In
other words, anything you allow to be allows *you* to be."

Val toggled back and forth between catching the
Kanes' meaning in one moment and in the next moment
losing the sense of their words entirely. She felt as if
she were looking out the window of an airplane. One
moment everything was shining and crystalline, the view
illuminated by the sun, and the next it was as if she had
entered a cloudbank and could see nothing. Luckily, she
remembered not to get lost thinking about it. She kept
listening instead.

It wasn't long before Val found herself being swept
away on the current of conversation. The evening
was humorous. The Kanes were engaging. The topics
ranged from getting to work on time to childcare, from
someone's eating habits to another person's relationship
with her boyfriend. Val forgot all about her bosses sitting
in the room with her. She forgot that she was new to this.
She felt as if somehow, she had come home.

As the evening wound down, Val was feeling relaxed
and refreshed. *That's pretty neat,* she thought, especially
since it had been a busy day. The weekend flew by and
soon it was already Sunday and the seminar was drawing
to a close. Before everyone left that night, Shya made a
remark that she would remember later, while at the time
it was just a concept.

"Transformation has happened here this weekend," Shya said. "We have all been here together and engaged in what has been happening. We know that many of you have already been talking about things you've noticed, but you won't actually see the depth of what has happened for you until you go back into the normal routine of your day. It's like a pebble that has been dropped into a pond. The rings go out into your life and you see what has transformed in retrospect. Pay attention. You just may be surprised by what you discover."

The next Monday morning Val exited the PATH train and found herself humming. It had been months since she had been so relaxed on the way to work. She found herself thinking about her day and felt a sense of excitement about the projects on her desk. Before she knew it, she had rounded the corner and her legs were striding in a purposeful manner toward the vestibule of her building, effortlessly carrying her forward to her day ahead. It wasn't until she was passing "the man" leaning against his doorframe that she realized that she had forgotten to avoid his leering stare and obtrusive comments. Just as he began making some kissing sounds, she abruptly stopped mid-stride and turned and looked at him. "Good morning!" she blurted, shocked to discover she really meant it. "Uhh…Good morning!" he stammered in reply.

In that moment, Val realized that she had never really looked at this man whom she thought had terrorized her all these months. She had been so busy keeping her head down and resisting his comments that she had created him to be a larger-than-life bully, a mean and menacing presence, a skeevy, leering pervert whose job in life was to make hers miserable. In reality, he was barely more than a boy, complete with acne. Unsure of himself, he blushed. She became aware that this young man was as insecure as she had been – more perhaps. A grin spread across her face and then over his. A connection was made. A moment of sweetness passed between them.

That day was a new beginning. From then on they weren't exactly friends, but they were two strangers who casually enjoyed the passing moments when their lives brushed one another's.

As Val sat down at her desk that morning, she recognized that she had just had a spontaneous experience of "wealth as a lifestyle." When the Kanes had posed the question, "What is Wealth?" on Friday night, she never imagined that having the freedom to walk down the street without being afraid or being hassled would become one of her new definitions. Her sense of excitement suddenly returned as she realized that she had just had a direct experience of Instantaneous Transformation. She hadn't planned it – it had just happened. Smiling to herself, she got down to work. Val had no idea how the events of this morning had come about but she was profoundly grateful that they had. She looked forward to next Monday night with the Kanes and could hardly wait to see what would happen next.

6

THOUGHTLESS PAINTING

At one of our *Say YES to Your Life!* Monday evening seminars in New York City, a young man named Gio stood up to speak. He has a wealth of black hair and was wearing a bold plaid wool shirt over black jeans with daubs and smears of bright-colored paint on the thighs. His sturdy work boots were speckled with color, also. It was the Monday following one of our weekend courses that Gio had attended, along with many other people from around the world. As he began to speak, we were taken by his vibrancy, his clarity and the alacrity with which he was expressing himself.

"I'm Gio and I am an artist," he began. "I took the Kanes' *Transformation in the Workplace* seminar this past weekend and wow! Last night I went down to my studio to work on a painting. It's a large jungle scene and I had the urge to do a big bold stroke on it. This is a risky move because the painting is already well-developed, so if I do something on it that doesn't work, it would...." Gio's voice trailed off as he looked at his audience in a rather stricken manner. You could see on his face the devastating effects of ruining a piece of art so near to completion. Then he laughed and we all laughed with him.

"But I didn't think," he said. "I just took the paintbrush and made the move and it was fantastic! I didn't worry or second-guess myself. I just created. Then I moved on to a different type of painting I am in the midst of doing. It is a realistic style of a man's face. The work was very detailed and precise. I needed to paint his facial hair. So I took a brush and applied the color in a spot to represent the pore and then did a quick stroke to create the hair itself. I didn't look at the big picture. I was just there for each hair and the image took on a life of its own and the face emerged but I didn't have to worry about what it would look like when I finished or if I was doing it right. It was a very thoughtless painting," he said with a grin.

"Today I was in the subway," Gio continued. "The sights were three-dimensional. The sounds of the people and the rushing train and the lights and the smells were all so rich and wonderful. When I left the subway station and stepped outside, I was taken on a visual rollercoaster, watching the leaves on the early fall trees being blown in a beautiful cool breeze.

"I also work for a famous artist during the day," he continued, "and I was cleaning his studio and stretching canvases. Every little bit of it was vibrant and alive. Normally I talk to myself about what I would rather be doing or about how to go about the things I already know how to do. But today was different. I was just being – and I felt amazing."

As Gio continued to speak, Shya suddenly realized that after more than forty years of exploration, his dreams had come to pass. In an instant, he recalled the springboard that had sent him on a wholly unexpected trajectory that had now come full circle.

EIGHT MINDLESS HOURS (AS TOLD BY SHYA)
It was the fall of 1961. Richard Alpert, who eventually became known as Baba Ram Das, and Timothy Leary were studying the effects of LSD at Harvard. LSD wasn't yet a banned substance when I was a student at New York University and the people I hung out with were interested in the psychedelic experience about which Alpert and Leary were writing.

I'd lived in Hawaii for eight months and on my way back, I stopped to see a young lady at Berkeley. She was attending a graduate program at the University of California. Her name escapes me after all these years, but she told me about having used LSD and the "magical" experiences she'd had with it. She told me to keep in mind that if I took it, it was a drug and it would wear off. So when I got back to New York, I got a sugar cube that was laced with "acid." I held onto that sugar cube for about three months, trying to figure out if I really wanted to take it and if I did, when and where.

At the time, I had a friend named Richard Green who lived on Manhattan's Lower East Side, 7th Street between Avenues C and D. The day came when I decided it was time and I wanted somebody to be with, so I contacted Richard and asked if I could take the acid trip in his apartment. He said, "Yeah, Terri and I are just hanging out, come on over." And I did. When I arrived I took the LSD and waited to see what would happen.

The first thing I felt was a heightened sense of non-verbal awareness. It was as if I could read the thoughts of Richard and his girlfriend Terri who were fighting and I'd never noticed that before. In other words, the subtleties of their bickering had been so normal to me, I hadn't been aware of them. But in this altered state of consciousness, they became apparent.

After being there for a couple of hours I decided to leave. I walked through the streets of the Lower East Side and I noticed people's faces. I could see the fear and upset that most people seemed to be living with. At that time, I felt most secure around New York University so I headed there. The closer I got, the more people seemed OK with themselves. It was as if I had come through an area of danger on the Lower East Side and at that time, it was rather dangerous, a high crime area. I moved into a zone of well-being as I got closer to the University and I wandered through the park at Washington Square and continued to look at people.

The smells, the sounds and the colors were three-dimensional and bright. Everything was crisp and I was simply observing it all. There was immediacy to my experience and it felt neutral. It was all new, all alive and I was not talking to myself about alternatives to what I was experiencing. I was just there as a silent witness, a participant in how my life was showing up. I can't say that I was simply an observer since that implies a distance or being removed from the situation. Rather, I was deeply observing, experiencing, living what was happening in each moment directly and without commentary.

It was as if the cultural filters had been removed, the ones that comment on good and bad, preferable or not. These are the filters that drive you forward to a "better" destination, commenting on whether or not you're living your life correctly under the dictates of the particular society in which you have been raised. These filters allow us to see what we expect to see and what we are looking for. They are like a schematic or template that life passes through and then we interpret only certain pieces out of the whole of the experience. It's as if we're colorblind in a world of color. We can see only what we can see but there is a whole range of hue that is hidden from us by these automatic filter systems.

That acid trip threw me into another world of seeing which was outside the familiar, one in which I wasn't talking to myself in my head. Rather, I was experiencing each moment directly, not second-guessing myself and not berating myself for how I thought I should be. I didn't realize all this at the time. I saw it more in retrospect, when after about eight hours, that internal dialogue of complaint and disagreement came back into my thought processes. It was a loud, haranguing voice, booming and intense after the experience of being so present in my life for eight hours without complaining or bickering or being right about anything. During that brief respite from my mind, I don't recall talking to myself or that my thoughts included words. I just was.

When it was over, I realized that there was another way or possibility of being. I wanted to recapture that presence. I wanted to live directly and feel in sync with my life and my surroundings. I wanted to be able to access the moment and not be thrown there as a result of a drug trip. And so I began the journey. I started investigating meditation and yoga and martial arts as ways to get into that moment-by-moment state of being that I'd briefly experienced under the influence of LSD.

It became a passion of mine that has determined my life's path. A quarter of a century later, I was spontaneously able to regain that space of being where I experienced life directly, knowing I was exactly where I should be. But this time, it was a natural occurrence and not one induced by drugs. Since then my life has been devoted to sharing this possibility with others.

I sat back and watched Gio that Monday night. As he delighted the folks in the room who were listening and did his best to articulate the essence of living in the moment, this moment of now, I realized that I had been successful. Gio was on a journey of his own to share this possibility, also. He had accessed this moment and the genius that is usually locked away behind a wall of self-recrimination and self-doubt. For him, Instantaneous Transformation had been an easy, effortless, drug-free event.

7

STRESS

*P*eople are born into cultures that have stress as an expected component to the gestalt of the culture itself, so it is part of their cultural download. While many people do things to reduce stress, such as yoga, meditation or exercise, most of them never stop to take a look at the mechanics of how it is produced. For those who do question what produces stress, the answer they come up with is usually inaccurate as it points to circumstances outside of oneself as the cause.

Experiencing stress in day-to-day life is not caused by circumstances. If it were, then Kat whom we spoke about in the previous section, *I Love Airports!*, would have had to have been stressed when her flight was cancelled, but she was not. **Stress happens when you say No to what is happening in your current circumstances.** For instance, if you are in the midst of doing something and the phone rings and you think of it as an interruption or intrusion, you will immediately feel stressed. Stress also comes from the need to be right that things should be different than they are. In the previous example, you are right that the phone shouldn't be ringing and that the caller is disturbing you. Stress happens when you think the moment isn't perfect as it is. It happens when you are trying to get somewhere rather than be where you are, as if getting somewhere is better than being here. It happens when you manipulate the circumstances to get what you think you want. Stress also happens when you are not being honest about something – when you are doing things that are outside of your own integrity.

THE THREE PRINCIPLES OF INSTANTANEOUS TRANSFORMATION AND STRESS

There are three simple ideas that are a great support structure, that allow you to re-center yourself when you find yourself stressed or when life seems to be operating against you. We call them The three Principles of Instantaneous Transformation. Why we call them "instantaneous" is that in the moment you identify where you are without judging yourself, you are already back centered – in an instant. It doesn't take time. It takes the willingness to discover where you are and how you are being, while giving up being right about what got you there. It takes giving up blaming yourself or others. The three principles are great tools that allow you to regain your equilibrium when you find yourself stressed.

Let's define these three principles and talk about them in relationship to stress.

The First Principle of Instantaneous Transformation: What you resist persists and grows stronger.

Resisting a situation is like exercising a muscle because resistance makes a muscle stronger. It also makes unwanted situations, emotions, or conditions stronger. In effect, ***the act of resisting something keeps it in place.*** When you resist something you have to push against it. And when you push against it, you get stuck to it so you can't let it go. Not wanting something to be the way it is, wishing things were different, trying to "get over" something, are all forms of resistance. They are also versions of saying No to the way your life is unfolding.

**The Second Principle of Instantaneous Transformation:
No two things can occupy the same you at the same time.**

When you are focused on something, everything else falls away. For example, we were once walking down a hill when we came upon a thorny rose bush that extended over the sidewalk. We paid attention as we walked past it so we wouldn't get snagged.

On our return trip up the hill, we noticed that on the road, right in front of that rose bush was a large truck with a horse trailer attached. We hadn't noticed it on the way down the hill and by the amount of pollen that had gathered on the windshield, it was clear that it had been parked there for some time. Earlier, when we were consumed with the bush, we didn't see the truck and trailer even though it was so close we could have reached out and touched it. And so it is with stress. Sometimes people are so consumed with stressors, they miss the rest of the world even though it is within reach.

**The Third Principle of Instantaneous Transformation:
Anything you allow to be, allows you to be.**

Let's go back to the first principle: Anything you resist persists and grows stronger. If you remove your focus from what you don't like, don't want or wish to be different and bring your attention neutrally back to what's in front of you, in that instant you're free. Stress-free. Yup, it's that simple. If you want to be "right" about someone else being "wrong," then guess what? You get stress, stress and more stress and in truth, you are stressing yourself. *Being stress-free is as simple as being where you are without disagreeing with your life circumstances, or saying No when life does not meet your preferences.*

8

WHAT ARE YOU FOCUSING ON? (AS TOLD BY ARIEL)

*H*ave you ever noticed that what you turn your attention to becomes your worldview? So if you are focusing on your complaints, then they become your reality. If you are worried about how you are doing, you become blind to the world around you. However, if you put your attention on the things in your environment, then your concerns resolve themselves on their own. Surprising things can become obvious if you simply pay attention to apparently inconsequential moments. Such was the case for me some time ago when I went with Shya for a short vacation far from home.

On the South Pacific coast of Costa Rica near Drake's Bay is a little ecotourism hotel, Poor Man's Paradise. Very remote, the only way to arrive at the hamlet is via a "surf landing," a ride through the waves on a skiff that drives up onto the beach. Shya and I went there on the recommendation of a friend who told us that the hotel had a wonderful boat and captain, perfect for a deep-sea adventure with a fly rod.

We fished for several days and on our last day we went far out to sea. The captain and mate were as eager to be on the ocean as we were, in search of sailfish and marlin and whatever else the watery world would provide. That day the fish were plentiful. We also saw dolphins cavorting and we rescued a large sea turtle that had gotten tangled in some of the detritus floating far off shore. Reluctant to come in, we ranged farther from the hotel than the captain had realized and so we returned by starlight with Shya and me lying on the deck gazing in wonder at the profusion of glittering diamonds flung across the sky.

The surf landing by skiff was a tad unsettling in the dark but we pulled up on the beach in fine shape, albeit wobbly legged and worn out from the sun and the wind and a full day spent out on the ocean. Giddy and exhausted, we hauled our equipment to our bungalow and left it at the foot of the steps because the power was out. Leaving our things, we followed one of the staff to dinner, guided by the light of their flashlight bobbing along. We were amazed by the profound darkness on either side of the path and were happy to arrive at the little candlelit dining area for pan-fried fresh red snapper and rice.

After dinner we got ready to haul our equipment to the room in order to begin packing our things. We were due to leave in the morning at five o'clock and we didn't relish the thought of getting up at three to round up our belongings without the aid of fresh coffee. However there was still no power and we had no flashlights. One of the staff was kind enough to loan me a headlamp and I was happy to slide it on and switch on the light. Weary from the day, my arms full of gear, I climbed to our second floor bungalow and entered our room. In that moment, something funny happened that has stayed with me for years.

I could suddenly see. *Why did I think it was dark? I can see over here*, I thought as I turned my head to the right corner of the room. *I can see over here*, too, I thought as my head swiveled to the left. *It's bright in here!* And then I laughed. Of course I could see. Whatever direction I turned my gaze, the headlamp automatically followed since it was strapped to my head and wherever I turned my attention, the view was illuminated. Then the light accidentally slipped, pivoted down into my eyes and I was blinded. It was a simple matter of readjusting the direction of the beam so I could go about packing my things.

That night in Poor Man's Paradise, I learned an important lesson. I realized that it is as if we have each been equipped with a personal headlamp that illuminates things. We see whatever we direct our attention to, allowing us to take care of the things and the people in the world around us. However, if our "light" slips and we focus on ourselves and how we're doing, we become virtually blind and lose our way. *With awareness, it's a simple matter of readjusting the direction of the beam away from our complaints, worries or thinking about ourselves and bringing it back to this moment of now and the world around us.*

YOUR MIND IS LIKE A SAUSAGE MACHINE

Most of us have eaten sausage of one type or another: a simple hot dog, a spicy Italian or even one made from tofu. The contents of a sausage may be different but each one has a casing that holds the contents together.

Our minds are like sausage machines. They grind up the circumstances of our lives and stuff them into a casing. Two people may be in nearly identical circumstances, but while one person's life is a complaint-filled trial, the other's is a delightful adventure. The difference is the casing or the context in which you hold your life and life circumstances, created by the thoughts that you believe to be true or believe to be "you." It's all about the way you approach life.

When you meet your life with a Yes even when the circumstances of your day show up radically different from what you would prefer, you can be present and feel well in yourself. The trouble is that most of us are well-versed in objecting to the minutia of our lives – like getting delayed at the airport, standing in lines at the supermarket and being stuck in traffic. We've been taught to socialize by complaining about the weather or by talking about how someone "did us wrong." But when you discover that this moment is perfect, then that reality becomes the casing for the sausage called your life.

9

IS THIS MY SHIRT... REALLY?

*I*n the summer of 2013, we were in Cambridge, England, leading a series of seminars when Shya unexpectedly had a dramatic episode that we later discovered was an extremely rare condition. Other people who went through this type of episode have generally viewed it as a deeply upsetting, fearful event. But fortunately for the two of us, being present and taking things moment-by-moment had prepared us to deal with this circumstance with humor and ease. This is what happened from Ariel's point of view:

Many of us dream about having the ability to live in the moment, to drop our story and discover the world anew. Shya and I had that experience. Well, Shya did, but that doesn't mean he remembers it.

It started on a Wednesday in Cambridge, England. Shya and I were scheduled to lead a seminar about Instantaneous Transformation for a local group that evening and we had some "afternoon delight" followed by a nap. We thought we would feel refreshed, but it didn't work out the way we had planned.

We were lounging in bed, enjoying a bit of post-coital languor, drowsy and sated and drifting toward sleep. Lying on our left sides, I had placed Shya's hand on my shoulder. Several weeks prior I'd had shoulder surgery and I was still feeling its effects. His hand was warm and soothing on the ache and our conversation would have been largely forgotten had things not taken a sharp turn.

"Ariel," Shya said, "when you had your shoulder surgery, I know we spent the night in an apartment but I can't remember where it was."

"Neither can I," I replied.

"How did we get that apartment?" he asked.

"Through the hospital."

"What was your doctor's name again?"

"Dr. Glashow," I said. I was warm and cozy and the conversation was slow and easy.

"I don't really know where I am right now," Shya said.

This was not a particularly unusual statement. We travel so much we may go to sleep in three different locations or countries on three subsequent days. When we wake up, we have to remember the room, the surroundings and the city we're in. It isn't disconcerting. It's more like emerging from a fog into the clarity of who we are in a particular time and space.

"Where are we?" Shya asked.

"In Cambridge," I replied drowsily.

"Cambridge?"

"Yes, Cambridge, England."

"What are we doing here?"

"We're doing a group here tonight."

"We are? How did we get here?"

By now I was beginning to perk up a bit as I realized that Shya's questions were somewhat odd yet sincere. "You know," I said. "We flew in from Helsinki. You just spent a week in Russia."

"Russia! Me? No. What was I doing in Russia?"

My eyes flew open and I quickly sat up. For an entire year Shya and I had planned a salmon fishing adventure in Russia, but in the months preceding the trip, our plans had radically changed. I had developed a condition called "frozen shoulder," an extremely painful affliction, and I was advised by Dr. Glashow that I would still be in no shape to go, so our friend, Peter, took my place. Shya and Peter had gone together and Shya had tied fishing flies for months prior to the trip. From the questions Shya was asking, I knew something was seriously amiss.

"You went to Russia to go salmon fishing," I said staring at him.

"No. Really?"

"Yes, you went with Peter, remember?"

Shya's mouth dropped open and the look on his face was incredulous. "Peter?!" he blurted out. "Peter? We went to Russia with Peter?"

"No, I couldn't go because I had shoulder surgery," I reminded him.

It was clear that something was desperately wrong. "Hang on, Shya," I said. "You might be having a stroke. I'm going to get you a baby aspirin."

I jumped up and began rooting around on the desk until I found the little snack bag filled with Shya's vitamins that contained a baby aspirin. I'd heard that if someone was having an episode, taking a baby aspirin would act as a blood thinner and could make the difference between life and death. In the moment, I couldn't remember if this applied only to heart attacks or also to strokes but I figured it couldn't hurt. I handed him a glass of water and put the aspirin on his tongue. "Here, drink this," I said as I picked up the phone and dialed "0."

"Front Desk, this is Vanessa."

"Do you have a doctor here?"

"No but we can get one. Do you need an ambulance?"

That question caught me off guard. "I don't know," I said. "My husband is extremely disoriented."

"I can get you an ambulance if you need one," she exclaimed. I heard a resounding click and looked at the phone in my hand. "She hung up on me!" I said.

Assuming she was calling the doctor or ordering an ambulance, I started getting us ready.

"I'm confused," Shya said. "Now, where am I?"

"You're in Cambridge, honey."

He paused and said, "I'm confused. What just happened?"

"We're in Cambridge to lead a group...."

"Really?"

"Yes. We had sex."

"We did?"

"Yes, and suddenly you got disoriented."

The phone rang. The ambulance was on its way.

"Let's get you dressed," I said, pulling on my own clothes. "I'm getting your underwear."

"I have underwear?"

"Yes, how about jeans?" I asked as I pulled a pair off a hanger.

"Jeans would be fine."

Shya had slipped into his underwear and I pointed to the shirt he'd been wearing earlier. "Put on your shirt, sweetheart."

Shya lifted the slate-grey long-sleeved t-shirt. It was a brand he had researched prior to the Russian trip, made of lightweight wool that would keep a person warm in winter and cool in summer. He'd been wearing it almost like a uniform, but now, he held the t-shirt in two hands as if he'd never seen it before. His face took on a look of wonder.

"Is this *my* shirt...Really?"

"Yes, Shya. Put it on," I said evenly.

Shya pulled on his shirt and I got him his socks and shoes and I got my own.

"I'm confused. Now where are we?" he asked.

"We're in Cambridge," I said.

"We are?"

"Yes. We had sex and then you became confused. The ambulance is on its way. You just came back from Russia where you were fishing for salmon."

I kept up a steady stream of conversation as I grabbed my phone to call our friend Menna to alert her that we would not be able to make the event we were scheduled to lead in just a few hours. Suddenly I felt as if I were operating like Menna and her husband Artur. Earlier in the day, they were being loving and respectful to their toddler Oscar, even though he wasn't talking a lot just yet. I couldn't imagine them getting irritated with him when he grew into the repetitive-question phase so I patiently answered each of Shya's questions as if they were new and had never been asked before.

Menna assured me she would take care of things, not to worry (bless her), and she promised to bicycle over to the hospital to meet us.

"I'm confused," Shya said, standing in the middle of the room. "I see fly rods in the corner. That must mean something."

"Yes, you went fly fishing in Russia."

"Russia? Really? We did?"

"Yes. You and Peter went fishing in Russia."

"Peter? We went fishing with Peter!?"

We went through the series of questions and answers once again and for a moment I got tight. My tone of voice changed and it immediately translated itself to Shya who suddenly became slightly agitated. I became aware of my change in attitude and let it go without being hard on myself for having gotten disturbed in the first place. *Oh, well*, I thought with a slight smile, *he won't remember it in a moment anyway.*

Shya paused and then he said again, "I'm confused.

Now what happened?"

"It's alright honey. We had sex and...."

"Was it good sex?" He asked innocently.

Innocently is the only way to describe it. It wasn't an embarrassing subject. Of course it shouldn't be after more than three decades together. It was a simple question, sincerely posed by a sweet, sweet man who was my husband and yet....

"Yes, it was very good sex," I said, laying my hand on his cheek. It was odd that Shya was so himself and yet not. It was as if his life had been distilled to *this* moment. While he clearly had no history, not even immediate history, he still retained his fundamental self, his innocence, his wonder, his love, his heart.

There was a knock on the door. It was the receptionist, portable phone in hand, which she gave me. She had been talking to the emergency operator who began by asking me a series of questions. The operator wanted me to count Shya's breaths, to say "now" each time he inhaled. I asked Shya to sit on the end of the bed and he obediently did so, waiting for what came next, although I suspect he wasn't actually waiting for anything. He was lost in a state of being or perhaps in stasis. I couldn't see his breath clearly.

"She wants me to count your breaths," I said.

In a childlike manner, he drew in a big lung-full and let it go.

"Now," I said and then we repeated the process and counted. The room phone rang once again. The ambulance had arrived. I said we would come down and they said no, that they would come to us. Of course that made sense. For a moment I had forgotten that Shya probably shouldn't navigate the stairs. He seemed so himself – yet not.

The two ambulance guys arrived. Chris, a man in

his mid-thirties with ginger brown hair and beard and Tom, slightly younger with a very round face, came into our room and began to assess the situation. "What happened?" Chris asked.

Shya said, "I'm confused. Now, what happened?"

"We had sex," I told Chris and Shya. "I went to the bathroom and when I came back, we started chatting and all of a sudden he became extremely disoriented."

"Where am I?" Shya asked.

"You're in Cambridge, England," I replied.

"I am?"

"Yes, sweetheart."

"I don't really understand what happened," he said.

"That's alright, honey, that's why these men are here."

That was when I became aware of something. Prior to the arrival of the EMTs, I'd been calm, directed and managing the situation as if it were urgent yet there was no panic, no emotionality. There was only this moment and actions to be taken to address what was unfolding before me. When Chris and Tom stepped in, that reality changed. During my initial conversation with them I started moving toward being less than capable. A quaver entered my voice. I was almost in tears. Perhaps, given the situation, this was expected. It was as if I wanted to abdicate responsibility to someone who "knew what to do" so I could let go.

I stood there for a brief moment and collected myself. I had started to become emotionally distraught by taking the first step down the road of "I want someone else to handle this, it's too much for me." I reeled myself back. (Thank goodness for all those years fighting wily fish.) I realized that getting panicked or emotional would only complicate things. I remembered that when I had briefly become agitated, it was passed on to Shya. So when Shya had asked me the same question for the tenth or twentieth time, I didn't say, "You're *still* in Cambridge. You've asked me that twenty times!" I simply listened to the question and answered it as best I could in that moment.

Chris asked Shya to sit once again on the end of the bed and he began to ask the standard types of questions to evaluate the situation. Asking Shya to remove his shirt, he squatted down in front of him and began to prepare the sticky pads to place on his chest for the portable EKG machine to monitor Shya's heart rate.

"Sir, how old are you?" he asked.

"Se...." Shya looked perplexed and gave me a look that seemed to say, *Help me out here, would you?*

"He's seventy-two," I said.

Stunned, Chris rocked back on his heels. I thought he might land on his behind. "No!" Chris said. "He can't be seventy-two. You aren't that old, sir. When is your birthday?"

Shya knew the answer to this. Like a youngster about to recite something he was extremely pleased to be getting right, Shya sat up proudly and with emphatic bobs of the head on all the appropriate syllables he said, "February 4, 1941."

"Wow, he looks great for his age," said Tom.

We were ready to go and I surprised myself by having the presence of mind to lock Shya's watch and wallet in the safe after removing his I.D. and insurance cards. I placed his shirt and jacket in a bag, donned my vest, grabbed my cell phone, money, my credit cards and the room key and we were on our way.

It was my first experience being in an ambulance. Shya's too, although he doesn't remember it. I was buckled into a seat on the left, facing the gurney where Shya was sitting up, strapped in. The ceaseless commentary and questioning continued. "I don't really know where I am," he said.

"That's alright honey, you don't need to," I said, brushing his hair from his forehead. "We're in Cambridge in an ambulance, heading to the hospital."

"What happened?"

I answered Shya's questions and carried on a conversation with Chris at the same time. He thought Shya might have had a stroke, but he encouraged me by saying that we were headed to Addenbrooke's, one of the best hospitals in all of England.

A few amusing or compelling moments during that ride have stayed with me. Shya pulled out the waistband of his jeans a few times and said with a sense of wonder and gusto, "I'm wearing underwear! You must have dressed me."

Chris told Tom to turn on the lights and the siren, assuring me that nothing was wrong but traffic was heavy and time might be of the essence. He was clearly worried and wanted to make sure Shya got to a physician as soon as possible. Somewhere along the ride, Chris stared at Shya's muscle tone, the definition in his shoulders, biceps, pecs and abs, and he blurted out, "How do you stay so fit?"

"Lots of sex!" Shya stated emphatically.

I choked back a laugh as Chris, clearly embarrassed, blushed. This was my husband, even if he didn't know who he was or where he was.

The next few hours were a bit of a whirlwind with blood samples, EKGs, taking his temperature, lights shined in each eye to judge his pupil response and a CT scan of his head. During this time, Menna arrived and it was a blessed relief to have a friend with me who knew the hospital system because she'd had her baby there.

"Menna!" Shya shouted with joy, "I know you!" Shya was clearly thrilled to see her, too.

As the hours went by, Shya's episodes of lucidity lengthened and he started remembering conversations for longer stretches of time. Instead of asking repetitive questions every minute, then every two minutes, it became a cycle of five minutes and more. But he was still hazy about what had come before. "Russia!? I was in Russia?" he asked once again when he was sitting semi-upright in the hospital bed in the observation area.

I had an inspiration. "I know how to get you to remember Russia," I said. "Remember the mosquitoes?" Shya and Peter had been there during mosquito season and had reported that the bugs had been fierce, especially in their sleeping quarters. I leaned close to Shya's ear and let out a high pitched whine, the annoying sound a mosquito makes buzzing your ear when you're trying to sleep. Shya became animated. Brushing at his ear to get me to go away, he said, "I remember Russia!" And he did...at least for the next five minutes.

Pretty soon, we began making jokes about having "mind-blowing sex," entertaining ourselves by watching his heart rate spike on the monitor when I kissed his forehead. As the afternoon moved on toward evening, I suddenly recalled that Shya had been in a slight boating accident in Russia. Both he and Peter had fallen backward and hit their heads when their guide got distracted and the boat hit a rock. I called Peter to get the details in case this was information that the doctors needed. When I handed the phone to Shya, he began to joke with Peter.

"What did you say your name was?" Shya quipped. We all laughed. "I'm coming back!" he said, clearly happy that his head was clearing. But in a short while, when he didn't recall having spoken with Peter, I realized we weren't out of the woods just yet.

Shya's doctors decided he should spend the night in the hospital so he could get a more comprehensive

MRI the following morning. They were mystified by his condition. Obviously there was a disruption in his memory, but each time they tested his strength, ability to move, lift his eyebrows, smile and frown, there were no telltale signs of physical impairment or drooping facial muscles that are common in stroke victims.

At about 9 P.M., when Menna and I got Shya dinner and brought it back to the ward, he said, "You came back!" in a childlike manner once again, clearly delighted to see us. After Shya finished his meal, Menna and I left for the night and although it was strange to be in the hotel room without him, I had a fairly restful night. When I returned early the next morning, Shya was finally back to himself, telling the nurses that an MRI wasn't necessary.

It turned out he was right. No MRI was needed. In the early afternoon, the neurologist arrived and asked Shya a series of questions. At the end of the examination the doctor said, "Right, then. This was a textbook case of Transient Global Amnesia. It happens when the blood flow to the hippocampus, the part of the brain that creates and stores memories, gets disrupted for a moment. It can happen to someone standing on the top of a ladder and reaching up with his head at an angle and straining. Or, like in this case, it can happen during intercourse. It's very rare and it's highly unlikely it will ever happen again."

Transient Global Amnesia? We had never heard of such a thing.

"That's it really," the doctor said. "You can go home now."

Shya was released and as we walked back down corridors that Shya didn't recall, we were giddy, like two school children given a reprieve and let out of class early. Our steps were lively, our hearts were light and things were easy between us as we grinned and joked about the effects of truly mind-blowing sex.

We went to see Artur and Menna and then we went out for a meal. It was great to have my husband back, but in truth, I never lost him. He had simply been distilled down to the moment and if I didn't run forward or back in time in my own mind, being with him was delicious.

This experience has left me at peace about our "old age." From time to time in the past, the unknown of the future had brought up some unease about how life would be and how I'd handle things if Shya were to become infirm. *Would I be OK?* I had quietly wondered. *What would it be like?* After I was thrown into the crucible of profound change, I discovered once again that I am much more than my story or any ideas I have about my own limitations. I also rediscovered the perfection of the moment and I surprised myself by how truly capable I am.

In the days and weeks following Shya's altered state, when we searched the web to find out more about Transient Global Amnesia, we found several stories where people described the experience as awful, extremely stressful, upsetting and frightening. Most folks who had TGA had become agitated and fearful and people who have heard Shya's story since have often asked me, "Didn't you freak out?" or "Weren't you afraid?"

It never occurred to me to worry, freak out or be afraid. Freaking out would not have helped the situation. Terrorizing myself with possible futures would not have indicated that I was more caring and it wouldn't have proved that I loved Shya more. It really is all about *Being Here*, and saying Yes to your life, regardless of the circumstances.

10

HONESTY

$\mathcal{B}$eing honest with yourself and others is an essential component to maintaining the experience of enlightenment. Transformation happens when you are honestly allowing your life to be exactly as it is in the current moment. ***If you manipulate things to get what you think you want, you are not allowing your life to take care of you.*** Your thought process, based in the culture in which you were raised, dictates your life. It isn't honest because it will do whatever it takes to get what it wants.

However, if you allow life to unfold the way it is happening, you don't have to manipulate things. Any manipulation to get what you want is a corruption of the current moment and it doesn't allow your universe to support you.

What you *think* you want is mind-based. It comes from the mind which only operates in a "more, better and different" modality. According to the mind, whatever you have isn't enough and you will always need something else that will make things better.

When you are driven to manipulate the circumstances to get what you want then you're not being honest with yourself. If you do anything that is dishonest to get what you want then you fall into the realm of survival, not transformation, and there is always the fear that life may not show up the way you would prefer.

Here is an example: If you manipulate your partner to say "I love you" by asking for it, or suggesting that they say it or hinting that you want to hear it, you will never feel truly loved. In your heart of hearts you will feel that you made your loved one say those words and you are likely to end up feeling even more insecure. It's a vastly different experience if he or she expresses love or kisses you without prompting.

INTEGRITY AND THE "LITTLE" THINGS

Most of us have been trained to sacrifice this moment in order to accomplish something, meet a goal or to get ahead. It's easy to get into the habit of shaving off the truth here and there in order to get what you want. But attending to the details allows life to become full. When you ignore your intuitive hunches, you are denying a truth and you are setting up a climate that is ripe for upsetting events, "mistakes" and drama. It is surprising how chipping away at the edges of your truth can break your structural integrity as a whole. Here is an example as told by Shya:

When I homesteaded in the Maine woods in the early '70s, we cooked on a wood stove and heated the house with firewood. I felled the trees and chopped the wood to keep a ready supply of fuel on hand for many a long cold winter and I became an expert at splitting logs. This is what I discovered: If I needed to split a big log, I set it on end, creating a flat surface to drive in a wedge or strike with an ax. But if I attempted to strike the center of the log, it resisted my efforts, the ax would get stuck and I would have to work very hard to remove it. However, if I simply sliced off a small piece of the edge, a bit of bark and a sliver of the interior, I broke the integrity of the entire log. Then it was ripe for splitting and a well-aimed blow would split the log in half.

I have found this to be a perfect metaphor for what happens when you sacrifice your integrity in little ways. When you have chipped away at the edges of your truth and life applies a little pressure, things easily fall apart. But when you operate with integrity, it is far easier to withstand life's pressures.

THE VAGRANT GIFT (AS TOLD BY ARIEL)

At age 14, I was a willowy little thing with long blonde hair and braces. Not yet old enough to drive, I was grown-up enough to ride the bus from our town of Gresham, Oregon, to downtown Portland for my orthodontist appointments. I liked going to Portland – it made me feel worldly and mature. On the way home I frequently stopped at the flower vendor for bright mini-carnations for a teacher or the school librarian – a little gift to give something back to those who were investing in me.

But on one bright spring day, I got a gift of my own from one of the most surprising sources. After my orthodontist appointment, with my braces newly tightened, I sauntered downtown several blocks to where I needed to wait for the bus back to Gresham. Even now, more than four decades later, I can still recall the bounce in my step and how the day felt so crisp, clean and ripe.

I breezed down the street to my corner, which bordered on a slightly seedier section of town. When I arrived, I leaned against the sun-warmed window, rested one foot on its sill and relaxed in the sunlight. I felt at ease, beautiful and in sync with the world.

While I was waiting for the bus, I noticed a vagrant ambling up the next block. As he crossed the street and headed my way, I felt curiously calm. He was a young man, probably in his early twenties, carrying a bottle in a brown paper bag. His pants were frayed, his old tan corduroy jacket had the cuffs rolled up, his light brown hair was scruffy. He repeatedly stopped folks on the street to ask if they had a bottle opener. Each individual he greeted veered away or backed up into a shop with an open door to avoid him. I remember thinking that something in this picture just wasn't right. This street person evoked such a strong reaction from passersby but to me he seemed non-threatening. Of course I was a teen and perhaps didn't register the real danger, but I felt as if his presentation was for show – a costume he adorned. I had no doubt that this young man was indeed a vagrant but somehow there seemed more to him than met the eye.

The fellow continued my way, repelling people left and right. As he moved past me, I was reclining in a perfect beam of sunlight shafting between the clouds. Suddenly he stopped, turned his head, his brown eyes fixed steadily on mine, and said, "Do me a favor. Just promise me you'll never rip anybody off."

Without thinking, I answered, "OK, I promise."

And there it was, a promise to a person I didn't even know that I would never steal from anyone. In a flash I recalled the two times I had stolen. Once, I had taken less than a dollar's worth of candy from Safeway. Another time, my girlfriend Judy and I had lifted a piece of red fabric with little white dots from a local store that she had turned into a halter top that I had happily worn. Suddenly I didn't feel so happy about that top.

I instinctively knew there was more to the story of this young man. Had innocent little childhood pranks of his own led him to where he was today? I looked up to watch him continue down the street but he was gone. No way could he have made the trip to the corner in that moment when my eyes were averted. I ran down the block, checking in each store as I passed. I made it to the corner and looked left and right but the mysterious young man had vanished.

Slowly I returned to the bus stop. My mind was awhirl with possibilities: Had I actually been lost in thought? – No it was only a moment. Was he an angel? Maybe he was someone sent by God with a message that I could ignore at my peril.

Whatever the reason, his words and my promise made an impact that I can feel to this day. The following week, I went to Safeway and gave them 87 cents for the stolen candy. I went to that little store and paid the $1.17 for that piece of fabric and had them wrap the receipt as a gift. I gave the package to Judy, telling her I was done stealing and that I had paid our debt. From time to time a teller at the grocery store undercharges me for the items in my cart and I make sure he or she puts it through again at the appropriate price.

The promise I made to this man and to myself is not one I have difficulty keeping. Perhaps he was an angel. Perhaps he was just a fellow who had lost his way and didn't want a pretty young girl to follow in his footsteps. All I know is that I am grateful for his advice. Being honest belongs to that clean, crisp spring day of my youth. It keeps things clean and crisp even now.

HONESTY AND MONEY

The email took us totally by surprise. We hadn't heard from Anne in close to five years. She wrote to us when we were in Hamburg, Germany, completing a series of courses there. Her email said, "I still owe you the course fee from my Costa Rican Adventure 2010! I looked on the Internet and I saw that you are in town. Then I looked up how much my tuition would be at today's rate and would like to pay my debt! I would like to come to your Tuesday night seminar, if that is all right with you, and I can bring dollars or euros or could wire transfer it to your bank account, if you would prefer. Either way, I would love to come on Tuesday night if this is OK for you guys! Sending Lovely Greetings, Anne."

In 2010 Anne and her then-husband William had come to one of our courses in Costa Rica. Since we had been friendly with them for many years and they had been having "cash flow" problems, we extended to them a payment plan so that they could pay their tuition fee in the months following the seminar. However, during the course, the couple revealed that they had been being very dishonest – first with themselves and then with their family, friends and business associates. Anne and William were in debt – deeply in debt. They had borrowed from their parents, his sister, the bank. They owed back taxes and had mortgaged their home and business. In effect they had been living for some time far beyond their means without any plan in place to pay it back. In fact, neither of them, at that time, actually had a desire to pay for their obligations either. They had been buying new clothes, cars, frivolous household items and they were now attending a week-long course that they clearly couldn't afford.

The couple's revelation about their financial situation put us into a bit of a quandary. We cared for them deeply but it was inappropriate for them to continue what they were doing. We also realized that it wouldn't be within our integrity to allow them to pay us, given that there were people to whom they had owed money for far longer than the two of us. We sat down with the pair and had a frank discussion.

"We know you love our seminars and the community of people here, but you need to go and handle your finances. You are welcome to come back one day, if you want, but not until you repay us. But you can't pay us back until you take care of all the people you owe from before you obligated yourself to us. Once you pay your taxes, pay back your families and all the others you owe, then you can pay us. It would be unfair to them for us to take your money while they are waiting."

We had no hard feelings with either of them but we were fairly certain that we would never see the thousands of dollars that Anne and William each owed us. We also realized that extending a payment plan to them had not done them any favors in the first place and have since made it a company policy to allow participants to attend a course only if they have paid in full in advance. As time went by we heard from friends that the couple was struggling and eventually that they had gotten a divorce. Years went by. So, it surprised and delighted us to hear from Anne.

When Tuesday night arrived so did she. Anne looked happy, fit and radiant. With a smile she handed us a present, wrapped in red paper with a green ribbon – her course tuition paid in U.S. dollars. On it she had written: *Thank You!*

That evening she was wholeheartedly greeted by the two of us and by friends, many of whom she also hadn't seen for years. Then as the course unfolded she did something amazingly brave. She stood up and told everyone about her journey.

"Hi, my name is Anne and I am so happy to be here tonight after a five-year hiatus."

She told everyone about coming to Costa Rica with us. She spoke about realizing the scope of her debt and her irresponsibility with money in particular and her life in general. She said that things became very clear once she looked at her life in a nonjudgmental manner and honestly saw what she had been hiding from herself.

Anne outlined our conditions of return, touched briefly on her divorce before proudly turning to us and saying:

"And I finally paid all my back taxes, too! It was a long road, but I had you both with me the whole way. You said two practical things that really stuck with me that helped to pull me through."

"Really," Shya said. "What were they?"

"First, you said 'The way out is in.' In other words, you discussed with me that in order to get out of debt and to turn the direction of my life around, I needed to get interested in all the ways I got there in the first place and that it was important that I did it in a nonjudgmental way. I had been resisting looking at all the ways I had been spending money. I hadn't wanted to see it at all."

"Let's talk about the Three Principles of Instantaneous Transformation for a moment, Anne," Ariel said. "First Principle is: What you resist persists and grows stronger. The more you resisted looking at your finances and how you were relating to money, the more the debt grew and the harder the situation became."

"Absolutely!" Anne agreed. "I had simply ignored that I owed money to everyone. I really didn't want to have to wait to get things. I wanted what I wanted when I wanted it. It was very childish really. But at the time I hid it all from myself and pretended that I was responsible, all the while imagining that my money situation wasn't a problem. Of course, the more I resisted looking at the truth the deeper in debt I became."

"That's a perfect example of the First Principle in action." Shya said. "Now the Second Principle is that you can only be exactly as you are in any given moment. So Anne, could you have looked at your way of spending money and your debt a moment before you did?"

"No, absolutely not."

"Could you have not been in debt in the first place?"

"No. That was such a relief to realize that I didn't have to go back and blame myself for what was already done and couldn't be changed. I also didn't have to look over the situation and blame my husband either."

"Perfect." Shya continued. "The Third Principle of Instantaneous Transformation is this: Anything you see without judging completes itself in the moment you see it. Of course, this didn't mean that when Anne actually looked at how she had been spending money that the debt 'completed itself.' Clearly she still had to be aware of her spending and had to do the work to make money and pay the debt."

"Shya and I once put our heads in the sand, so to speak," Ariel said, "and overspent against the advice of our accountant when we built our conference center in Bali, Indonesia. When we came up for air and were honest with ourselves about the situation, we quickly became very clear about the things we really needed as opposed to the things that we merely wanted. For example, it was important for me to realize that a shirt that was on sale for twenty dollars, was still twenty dollars that I could put toward paying back my obligations."

"Exactly!" Anne said.

"What was the second thing that stayed with you?" Shya asked.

"Well Shya, I have heard you and Ariel often say that relationship is not a 50/50 deal, that I was 100 percent responsible for my life and the health of my relationship. You said that I could either be the victim of my life or the author of my life.

"At first I was such a victim about everything, which made things so difficult. I was so angry – angry at myself, at my husband, at the situation and at the world. But I kept hearing your voices in the back of my head saying something like, 'You couldn't have done it any differently than you did. It's over. Now what?'

"When I really looked and faced my part in getting myself into debt and in my relationship falling apart, then I was finally able to forgive myself and then everything changed.

"As you know, I now have gotten a divorce from William. But I realize that I am responsible for how my relationship turned out and it's not his fault."

"We often say that it takes two to fight and one to end the fight and that person always has to be *you!*" Shya said.

"Things are really easy between William and me," Anne said. "I don't hold any resentment against him at all."

"It sounds as if you don't hold any resentment against yourself either, Anne, which is a perfect definition of responsibility. Responsibility is not about blaming anyone – even yourself. It really is about being accountable for the state of your life. When you see yourself honestly and don't judge yourself then you can take appropriate actions without all the heaviness of self-doubt and guilt."

"Yes! It was the greatest gift for me to discover that there is nothing wrong with me and that nothing needs to be fixed. It took me awhile, but I paid everything back and I am now really thankful for everything."

Anne has always been a tall woman, since she stands at least six feet. But on that night, it was the first time we had ever seen her look really tall in stature. It was as if by being honest with herself and taking actions to handle what she saw, she had finally grown into her frame and matured into the brilliant person that had only been a distant potential before.

11

IT'S ALL ABOUT
THE LITTLE THINGS

*I*f you practice being here for the minutiae, big things won't seem so big and you'll be ready to meet what comes moment-to-moment. *Life never gives you more than you can handle.* Being right here to experience what is happening in this moment, whether it seems to be packed with meaning or seemingly inconsequential is key. At times, you'll lose yourself in thought or in forward momentum as you go about getting things accomplished – but no matter. As soon as you notice that you've been preoccupied, you're already back in real time. No need to chastise yourself or resolve to do better. Living a stress-free, drama-free life involves bringing yourself back to this moment without chastising yourself for having gotten distracted. Here is an example as told by Shya:

MISSING MY MORNING COFFEE
I love my morning cup of Joe. Coffee and I have been friends for almost as long as I can remember. When I was a kid, I used to drink from my parents' forgotten cups, pretending I was an adult. Coffee was my companion in college, company during late-night cram sessions. Coffee houses were the destination of choice

for my friends and me as we spent long evenings having deep, philosophical discussions about life – life we had yet to live. In later years, when Ariel and I got together, there was a progression of caffeinated times and those that were without. When we moved to our Park Avenue apartment in the '80s, there was a little bistro downstairs where we would have a morning cappuccino and a croissant or sugary pastry. There were years when we gave it up, but even in those times, Ariel and I still enjoyed the pungent aroma of coffee being freshly ground and brewed.

A few years ago, Ariel and I splurged and bought ourselves a lovely espresso machine that heats our cups, grinds the beans, and makes the espresso as strong or as light as we like. Since I like my espresso strong and hot, I pushed the appropriate button one morning and it pressed out a little cup of my favorite elixir. The cup was small, its contents strong. I took my first sip. Mmmm, hot, delicious – both the ritual of a morning cup and its smell and taste. Cup in hand, I set off to start my day. There were things to do and plans to be made. Shortly thereafter I looked down and magically, my cup was empty. I realized that I'd been lost in thought and tossed the coffee down as if it were water, oblivious to the taste, temperature, texture and the moment itself. My thoughts had been all-consuming and the moment was eaten by their magnetic force.

Smiling down at my cup somewhat wistfully, I realized that enjoyable things cease to be enjoyable if you aren't there to experience them. I couldn't go back and taste what I'd already drunk. I could make another cup but the caffeine I'd consumed had already worked its magic and I didn't need more at that moment. Returning to the kitchen, I washed my cup. It was time to move on with my day. It was a short but sweet reminder that if I don't want to miss my morning coffee, I need to be there while I'm drinking it, even if I'm not yet fully awake.

ACCESSING THE MOMENT

The mind plans. The mind thinks. The mind draws upon what it already knows, rearranging a finite set of data in an attempt to create something new. This isn't a problem. This is normal. In fact it's something people routinely do when organizing their days. But enlightenment includes something else. It includes accessing *this* moment rather than being lost in thought. It includes an active engagement with your environment and the people who inhabit it. It also includes saying Yes to how your life is currently unfolding rather than being fearfully preoccupied with worries from the past projected into a fantasy future.

Each of us is encased in a forward-thinking machine that references the past in order to improve upon what has gone before. And so, we fear the future, afraid of doing our lives "wrong," of making bad choices, of falling behind, of not getting ahead, not reaching our goals, of dying or enduring the death of a loved one.

When you're living in a state of fear, you are not accessing the moment. When you fall prey to your fearful mind and the machine that drives you forward, you lose your experience of the interconnectedness we all share. You lose sight of God Consciousness, your higher self, your connection to the Vedas, to the oneness of all – depending on how you wish to view or term it.

You have the potential at any given moment to be in sync with life and with the universe at large. Your universe is taking care of you right now and it's going to take care of you in the future. You never need to scheme, connive or manipulate to make it work out the way you think it ought to be or the way you would prefer. The current moment of now is perfect and you don't need to be different than you are to survive it.

The challenge is that we've all been raised in cultures based in survival. The forward-thinking nature of our cultures drives us toward future fulfillment or satisfaction that is never forthcoming because it dismisses the current moment in favor of some future "better" moment. When you strive to achieve what you *think* will be better, there is no satisfaction because all you have is the current moment. Even if you achieve your goal, satisfaction will elude you because this moment leads to the next moment, which leads to the next moment and if you're dissatisfied right now, the future will arrive as an extension of your current dissatisfaction. You are dissatisfied whenever you think that something else in the future will be "it," and what you have or where you are isn't "it."

The simple truth is that the current moment is all there is. The technology of Instantaneous Transformation allows us to step out of that survival dynamic if we choose to and discover a creative lifestyle – one in which we're not only driven to achieve and accumulate wealth but one where we can also experience our lives. The game of self-realization, of living a transformational lifestyle, requires us to retrain our values. It involves reining in our predisposition to strive for a future fulfillment so we can appreciate what is happening in life right now. The mechanical predisposition to upset and irritability can be dissolved if you honestly see it and feel it without blaming the circumstances for how you feel. It is about being in the midst of whatever is happening rather than doing anything about it. This "being here" allows for the completion of your forward-thinking nature. All it takes is a moment to be in sync with your life once again. All it takes is saying Yes to how your life is showing up – right now, even if circumstances are not meeting your preferences...and even when they are.

HARRY'S PERFECT MOMENT

As he swung his legs over the side of the bed, Harry knew something was different, but he had no idea that today he would have a "perfect" moment. It was a Monday morning and he had just taken one of our weekend seminars, *Live in the Moment and Not in Your Thoughts.* Donning his cotton robe, Harry made his way to the kitchen and started his day like he always did by preparing breakfast for his wife and two young sons. He got out the usual supplies – knife, cutting board, bowl and fruit – and laid them on the butcher-block center island. Suddenly the morning took a new twist. There was a break in his routine. The "same old, same old" wasn't any longer.

In the past, Harry had dutifully made fruit salad for breakfast. He and his family always liked the end result but Harry had never enjoyed the process. He never liked the way the peel heaped up on the counter or how the juice ran off the board or the stickiness of his fingers or the slipperiness of the knife in his hand. It just wasn't elegant or sophisticated. Making breakfast wasn't fun or enlivening. It was a task to be accomplished so he could get on with his day.

That morning, things were different. Spontaneously, Harry was actually there for what he was doing. He wasn't trying to get it over with. He appreciated the texture of the fuzz on the skin of the kiwi, the scent of the strawberries, the color of the oranges and curve of the banana as he set them on the counter. Then he had an inspiration. Why not use the bowl he usually reserved for the salad to hold the peels? Harry began to peel the kiwi in a single spiral, enjoying the moment when the skin landed lightly in the bowl. He slid the knife through the succulent green fruit, marveling at the starburst pattern of seeds in each slice, spreading them in a cascade of color along the upper edge of the board. Next the banana. The peel also landed in the bowl and the slices ran in an orderly line beneath the kiwi. Soon his board was a rainbow of color with berries and oranges, melon and papaya. Discarding the peels, Harry rinsed his hands and the cool stream of water caressed his fingers.

Returning to the center island, he assembled the fruit in the bowl and lightly tossed it with his usual serving spoon. Looking at the finished product, he wondered if the salad was somehow more vibrant, its succulent fruit a riot of color. Taking a deep, cleansing breath, Harry paused as he realized that it was a perfect moment. He washed the fruit board and wiped the counter, feeling an unusual yet welcome sense of accomplishment, a calm serenity. As the day progressed, the sense of wonder stayed with him. His mind kept touching upon the memory of his morning: the colors, smells, his feelings, the tastes.

In the afternoon, Harry got out his bicycle, strapped on his helmet and pedaled off into the sunshine down the local streets on his way to work. It felt good to stretch his legs and soon he was moving at a clip. Unbeknownst to Harry, he was about to have another perfect moment. Life was about to present him with a shock. As he pedaled down the street, Harry flashed back on his morning. He recalled making the salad in his mind's eye, running through the details, savoring the perfection. His legs pumped in rhythm as his gaze turned inward and once again, fruit marched across his cutting board in colorful stripes. Suddenly Harry's bike lurched. In an instant he was pitched over the handlebars. Time slowed. Sights and sounds crystallized. A woman screamed. Head over heels, he saw the incongruous sight of an upside-down police car. Then he landed in a heap on the asphalt. People rushed to his aid but miraculously he wasn't hurt – just a few minor abrasions and a slightly damaged ego.

A short time later Harry stood on shaky legs preparing to resume his ride. The police officer and the good Samaritans had melted back into their own days and their own routines. If anyone had stayed there to watch, they would have seen a goofy grin spread over Harry's face as he had a series of rapid-fire realizations. The accident had been totally his fault. Lost in thought, reliving his "perfect" moment, he had hooked a pedal on the curb and it had pitched him forward. Standing safely on the sidewalk, Harry was stunned to realize that each moment was perfect – not just those he preferred. He saw that when he was rerunning the past, he was no longer present, no longer in this instant of time. By rehashing even a *perfect* moment, he had made himself accident-prone. After all, the course he had just taken was *Live in the Moment and Not in Your Thoughts*. He climbed back on his bike, this time aware of his surroundings. Yes, this morning had been lovely and special and profound but time and his life had moved on. Taking a deep breath of air, Harry had yet another perfect moment...and another...and....

12

NO PAIN, ALL GAIN

Self-discovery isn't meant to be painful. If it is, then you're working on yourself, lost in the story of your life, or simply resisting what is.

Most of us have been trained to think that we need to work on ourselves and that self-introspection, self-growth, is a painful affair where we delve into the deep dark recesses of our past and our personal story. Such was the case at one of our *Say YES to Your Life!* seminars in Manhattan. As we looked out at the participants, it was easy to spot a woman who looked lost. She was obviously working on herself and immersed in the story of her life.

Maria had sent us an email earlier in the day detailing how miserable her life was with an unsatisfying job, a child who was acting up, an unsupportive boyfriend, money challenges, and parents who were to blame for it all. As we introduced ourselves and how to approach the evening, she was alternating between being preoccupied and wanting to make sure that we knew she was upset. We suggested to the attendees that if they wanted to see their lives transform, it was simple and assured, provided they listen. It wasn't so much that we were about to impart profound words of wisdom. Rather the act of their being engaged, of listening to what another has to say from his or her perspective, would pull them into the moment – and when you're in the moment, your life transforms as a byproduct of being here. It's as simple as that.

As the evening progressed, Maria was more interested in the internal conversation she was having with herself than the conversation happening in the room. If she caught our eye, she was quick to show us that she was in distress, shaking her head, looking forlorn. In the meantime, several participants stood up to speak in front of the group and each one was more compelling than the last.

Eventually it was time to take a break. Folks lined up to speak with us, Maria in the lead. Tears ran down her face as she outlined her tale of woe. It's not that we were unsympathetic. We simply knew that the way she was going about things would cause her more pain, not less.

"Maria, you aren't really listening when people speak," Shya said.

"I am, too!" she quickly replied.

"No, I've been watching you," said Shya. "You're involved in a conversation with yourself and haven't been following what...."

"I am. I'm listening," Maria insisted. "You have no idea. I'm trying."

"We believe you," Ariel said. "We believe that you're trying your best but there is a level of listening that you haven't experienced yet. Try using your eyes and look at who's speaking. That way you're more likely to hear them rather than think about the story of your life."

Maria's eyes were diverted long before Ariel finished speaking because she was forming a rebuttal in her mind.

"No. I'm listening. Really I am. It's just that...." She launched into a replay of the story she had emailed us earlier in the day. It was as if she had hit the restart button and the tape had begun again. Words spilled from her mouth and tears spilled from her eyes. From her perspective, her life was wrong, the circumstances were unfair, she was a mess and her parents were to blame.

"Maria, perhaps our approach doesn't work for you," Ariel gently said.

"You want to get rid of me?! Perfect. That's the story of my life."

"It's not that," Shya continued. "It's just that our approach isn't for everyone. If you're determined to prove that the story of your life is true and that the past determines your life today, then our approach isn't for you. We have discovered that no two things can occupy the same Maria at the same time. You can either be here, in this room, or you can rehearse and rehash your story, which only reinforces it."

We spent more than half of the break speaking with her while the others who wanted to talk with us waited patiently.

"Respectfully speaking," Ariel finally said, "we need to take a moment with these other folks before it's time to begin again."

"We suggest that you get engaged with the people here on this break. Talk to them. Introduce yourself. Get interested," Shya said.

Maria agreed and backed away, her face crumpled and broken. She was lost in a tape loop of complaining and wasn't really where she was but we trusted that this was exactly where she needed to be and how she needed to be in that moment.

At the end of the evening, we took time, as usual, to chat with folks and answer their questions. We saw Maria in our periphery as she spoke with a couple and gave them each a hug. When she turned and approached us, she looked like a totally different woman. Her face was open, her countenance clear. Years had dropped away.

She was lighter, freer, alive.

"Ariel, Shya, I just discovered something," she said in a state of wonder. "I always thought that I had to tell my story over and over again to myself and to others in order to work my way through it. But all that does is keep it around and reinforces it. If I don't, it slips away."

Maria and her insights were a gift. She had thought that she needed to work on her past and talk about it with people as if that would somehow use it up. Her epiphany was the realization that the more she "worked on it," the stronger it became. The more she told it to herself and to others, the more well-formed, real and entrenched it became. Now she had spontaneously seen that if she stopped focusing on her problematic past and working on it, it was over and it lost its power over her life. Letting go of the story and moving on to living her life was all it took.

You can either get lost in the machinations of your mind, where you're attempting to do your life "right" and judging everything you do or don't do from within the parameters of right and wrong (which is exhausting and non-productive), or you can live your life. But we all have been trained to judge ourselves and how we are doing and we haven't been trained in allowing ourselves to be who we are and the way we are. We have an idea of where we need to get to and what we need to accomplish. What seems to hold us back is the story of our lives – all the reasons why we can't, all those past "failures" and the memory of them, our current complaints about what we have, juxtaposed against what we would prefer. We also have an idea that we have done it wrong in the past or how we are today is someone else's fault. For example, we have that notion that our parents are to blame or that they have "raised us wrong."

What if your life is unfolding perfectly in this current moment of now and there is absolutely nothing wrong with you? All it takes is to get here and to stop resisting being the way you are right now. This is difficult because our lives are dictated by scripts that were written before we ever arrived. We've been trained to act out these assigned roles, but becoming aware of the existence of the script allows you to extricate yourself from it, thereby enabling you to live your life, not the prescribed storyline.

For most of us, working on ourselves is so normal, we don't realize we're doing it and a life free of that self-deprecating thought process seems impossible. But the Second Principle of Instantaneous Transformation, that no two things can occupy the same space at the same time, creates the possibility of a life free of that socially prescribed dictate to get "better" as if you're not already OK.

You can start enjoying your life right now – the way it is. Not someday when you get your to-do list done. You don't have to wait. *This* moment of now really is all there is. Disregarding it for some fictitious future will result in your disregarding that future when it arrives. You might as well start appreciating this moment. It's all you've got. That's what Maria did. Her life circumstances and the story behind them had not changed a bit. She was simply no longer lost in re-reading that well-worn page of her internal script and she started actually living in the moment where her life was very satisfying. People frequently get the idea that they are somehow "broken" and they blame their parents for the current state or condition of their lives. This psychological perspective of cause and effect has been a socially acceptable way of relating to circumstances but it totally lacks personal responsibility and in fact, each human being is personally responsible for his or her own deeds and actions. It is a challenge to give up blaming one's parents because there is so much social agreement that they are responsible for how we turn out. And as long as people use their parents as a touchstone to compare their lives to, they will never be able to discover their authentic selves. As a result, the elusive state of inner peace will remain forever out of reach.

WHAT DOES IT COST YOU TO BE "RIGHT"?

Judge Judy is a television program in which one person sues another in a public court of law. This show is usually a blatant, exaggerated version of two individuals who are determined to be right. On *Judge Judy,* people are committed to proving that the other was a horrible landlord or tenant, an awful sibling, parent or child and that the person opposing them ruined their day, their health, their wedding or even their life.

Whenever we watch this show we see the cost of being "right." If you ask yourself the question, *What does it cost me to be right?,* we're sure you will spontaneously come up with an answer or answers.

Here are a few of the things that affect your well-being that happen as a result of being right:

You Have to Stop Listening. If you're being right, from your perspective the other person is simply wrong. This shuts down all avenues of communication. You can't listen to another's point of view when you're being right, as it may challenge your position. So "listening" is not really listening at all but rather a scheme to find ammunition for your arguments.

You Have to Be Defended. If you're being right, you have to defend your point of view, leaving no space for negotiation, compassion or true communication. When you're defended in one area, it also affects all areas of your life. Have you noticed that when you're in a fight with someone, it affects your ability to be intimate? Even if the disagreement is with someone at work, that conflict and defensiveness will follow you into the bedroom. Lists of their transgressions and arguments to justify your point of view can intrude during lovemaking and your ability to feel pleasure is diminished. Even in the height of passion there can be a sense of upset rumbling underneath where you are not totally available – part of you is busy maintaining your stance. If you truly get swept away in the moment, you'll have to give up your position that he or she is wrong and that you're right.

You Have to Withhold Your Heart. If you're being right, you have to withhold your heart lest you reconnect with the person or people you are fighting with and suddenly find compassion or see their point of view. In effect you hurt yourself or cut yourself off from your heart in order to maintain your position. Think about it: Most of us became very good at this when we were teenagers. We learned how to withhold our hearts and our love as a weapon to express our displeasure when our parent or parents had a rule we disagreed with or made us clean our rooms, do our homework or wouldn't let us have our way. Perhaps you gave them the "silent treatment" or shouted unkind things like, "I hate you!" Maybe you stomped around and slammed doors in protest. These strategies were done to make known that he or she was wrong and to hurt them or show how unfair they were being. But the real person you hurt was (and is) yourself.

In the next section, as told by Shya, he illustrates what happens when you get lost in a cycle of being right and also what can happen when you really, truly let go of that position. It also dramatically demonstrates the magic of apologizing and really meaning it, even when you have done nothing "wrong."

SEE DICK TRANSFORM

At 15, I got my first boat. Well, that was the fantasy. I didn't actually own a boat but I bought a used ten-horsepower Evinrude outboard motor and I would rent rowboats from Henning's Fishing Station at the foot of the Atlantic Beach Bridge. It was the summer I worked as a veterinarian's assistant. I begged my parents to loan me the money for the motor, promising them I would pay them back out of my earnings. I put in $100, they advanced me another $200 and I was good to go. Only problem was, I found fishing much more fun than working for that vet, so my poor folks never got their money back. I got myself fired and went fishing instead.

Forty years later, I actually bought a boat of my own. A friend took Ariel and me to a boat show in Connecticut where I was a kid again. I got to walk around on many different brands of boats – Sea Rays and Boston Whalers, Sea Pros and Makos – the stuff dreams are made of. Eventually, I ended up sitting on a beautiful little 22-foot Pursuit. It was an open, center-console with a raised front deck, a perfect platform for fly fishing which was, by then, my passion. Although the boat was sitting in a parking lot, I was already at sea in my mind, catching striped bass from the forward deck with a fly rod, making perfect casts to rising fish.

Ariel first knew that we were buying a boat for real when I sat on my Pursuit and didn't get off for an hour or so. It was a big family decision to invest in a boat, but she knew that my heart had been in fishing since I was a boy. When it came time to name the boat, each of us quietly, privately knew her name: *Shya's Dream*.

At first, it was quite a learning curve to pilot a boat. I

took a safe-boating course offered by the Coast Guard. Then my friend introduced me to the concept of "dock and goes" where we tossed a floating cushion out in the middle of the bay. Then I would attempt to approach this decoy as if it were an actual dock in different weather conditions until I became proficient at not bumping it or running it over.

Ariel and I didn't live near the water so we settled on docking our boat at Zuley's, a little marina down on the Jersey shore that was the closest one to our home. It sat near the mouth of the Raritan River, near Staten Island and it was only a short hop to the ocean.

Zuley's is on the edge of a little tidal creek and in the beginning I had to time my departure and return times for when the tide was not rushing in or out – slack tide. This restricted our coming and going to approximately one half hour out of every six. I was determined to master docking my boat in all conditions, so I spent many hours learning to compensate for the effects of the tide and wind on my craft. I was very proud of myself as I moved from novice captain to one who was able to maneuver my way during all types of weather and water conditions.

Four years later, we were up in Cape Cod and I sat on a new boat. It was a 28-foot Contender. And so the process began again. It was time for an upgrade. We soon became the proud owners of an "elderberry" colored boat. Actually, it was a dark creamy pink, but probably the manufacturer thought most men wouldn't purchase a pink boat so they gave it a fancy name. We named this one *Dream On.*

At this point in time, I still docked my boat at Zuley's. They had mooring slips on both sides of the tidal creek and I had my boat on a floating dock next to the main boat ramp and the marina itself. On weekends, there was a lot of traffic in and out of the marina and the owners hired Dick, a retired New Jersey State policeman, to sit near the dock, collect ramp fees and direct people where to park their cars and trailers for the day. Dick was actually an accomplished captain himself, but his health was somewhat fragile and I think it confined him to the shore more than he would have preferred. However, he was very good at helping nervous captains navigate the ramp, particularly when the tide was rushing.

One Saturday afternoon, I was backing my boat into my boat slip and Dick was sitting nearby. It was a tricky maneuver but by now I was very skilled at compensating for the water's speed and the wind's push, able to slip around other boats and the protruding dock. Dick hurried down to help me. Rushing to my aid, he began shouting instructions. Frankly, in that moment, I found his "assistance" an intrusion. It was a distraction from the tricky docking procedure I was attempting to undertake. Dick had no idea that I had made this move many, many times and that it was a source of pride for me how well I could execute the maneuver.

When I told Dick I didn't need his help, it came out more tersely than I intended. Pride collided with pride. Dick may have been a big man, six-foot-two and 250 pounds, but inside he was a sensitive youngster and I hurt his feelings. Neither Dick nor I realized how upset he was, but it eventually became apparent.

As I left the dock that day, I apologized for growling. "Humph" or something like that was the reply. Who knew that this was the beginning of a battle of wills that would last for two years?

The next year, my boat and I occupied another slip across the tidal creek, directly across from the boat ramp and Dick. One Saturday morning, early in the season, I came down to the marina and realized it was cold and rough outside. I wasn't too sure that I wanted to spend much time out in the choppy water, but since I had a new fly rod, I thought I would practice a little casting off my dock. Perhaps the weather and the waves would calm down in the meantime.

I was startled to hear a voice shouting from the other side, "Hey, get off the dock!"

I looked up and it was Dick. I shouted back, "Don't worry, Dick, it's me, Shya. I'm allowed to be here. This is my slip."

"No, get off the dock. Zuley doesn't want anyone up there."

"This is my boat and my boat slip. Zuley says it's fine, really," I hollered back. "Give Zuley a call and she'll tell you it's fine."

"No, get off the dock now or I'm calling the police!"

I could see he was very agitated and I decided to cut my losses and head for home. As I pulled out of the parking lot, I saw a police cruiser pulling in. Dick was upset, all right.

The next day I called Zuley. "Hey," I said, "Can you explain to Dick that it's OK for me to be on the dock? He was very upset with me yesterday and actually called the police when I was leaving because he thought I was trespassing."

Zuley apologized for the confusion and promised to talk with Dick.

The next weekend, the scene repeated itself. No police this time, but he yelled in my direction. I simply headed to my boat, started it up and went out on the water.

I called Zuley again. This time it was more of a complaint. "Zuley, can you please talk with Dick? He was harassing me when I came down to my boat."

"I'm sorry," she said, "he can get territorial. He's like an old guard dog. I'll talk with him."

It didn't matter what she said. Dick was like a dog with

a bone and he wouldn't let go. Zuley tried writing me a special pass for the dock, taping a permit to the bumper of my car, but to no avail. She couldn't fire him because he was reliable in other ways and she needed him. I began to come to the marina strictly during the week.

The following year, my boat slip was once again back on the marina side, near the boat ramp and near Dick. I tried different tactics to solve the situation. I tried apologizing. I thought if I told him I was sorry we could put this misunderstanding behind us and, if not be friends, at least be cordial. Dick wasn't interested. He claimed to have nothing going on with me. So basically, I nodded to him when coming and going but confined myself to that.

Soon, strange things began happening by my boat. There were mooring ropes that I used to secure my boat to the dock. These ropes were much longer than I needed so I coiled the extra next to the dock cleats. It looked crisp and kept the lines from being tangled and tripped over. However, there were many mornings when I would find the lines in disarray, dangling in the water. *What a nuisance*, I thought, and I would coil them up neatly once again on the dock. But they never stayed that way for long.

Eventually I began to notice a pattern. If I went out on a Monday, and went boating again on another weekday such as Thursday, my lines would be neat and coiled just like I had left them. However, when I came to the boat after a weekend, the lines were always tangled and dangling in the water, growing brown from silt and sea life. I suspected it was Dick, but it seemed so petty. He was a grown man after all. Perhaps it was kids coming by, or Zuley's young grandchild. I decided to give Dick the benefit of the doubt and keep my suspicions to myself.

The next time I went to the dock, I brought my drill

and some screws. After neatly coiling the lines, I secured them with a few screws and figured that this would make the lines less likely to be inadvertently kicked into the water and less attractive for a youngster to mess around with. But it wasn't long before the lines were ripped up, kicked around and in the water again.

This was not fun. It felt like someone had a vendetta with me. It definitely didn't seem random. It felt more personal. Could it be Dick after all?

Then one Sunday morning, I made it to the marina shortly after Dick had unlocked the gates, just as he was setting up his chair and sun umbrella, getting ready for his day. Once again the ropes were ripped up from where they had been screwed to the deck and had been tossed in the water, but this time there was a difference. They were still coiled. They hadn't been in the water long enough to straighten out. I knew I had the culprit. It was the next best thing to catching him in the act.

Once again I went to Zuley. "This is getting ridiculous," I complained. "Boating is supposed to be fun and relaxing and not stressful like this. I feel like I'm in a war zone."

Zuley defended Dick and I understood. If she really saw that he was vandalizing my dock area, she might have to fire him and then she would need to find someone new and Dick, with all his experience, would be hard to replace.

"I can't believe he would be so juvenile," she said. "He used to be a state cop!"

"But Zuley, that line hadn't been in the water more than ten minutes and he had just unlocked the boatyard with his key! Can't you just talk with him and ask him to leave me alone?"

She said she would. I sincerely hoped that things would ease after that, now that he had been clearly implicated in the trouble. Sad to say, I was mistaken.

The next time I went to take *Dream On* out for a spin, I came down to the boatyard on a Thursday. It was a quiet day. I looked forward to some rest and rejuvenation from our busy schedule. It was low tide and I walked down the ramp and once again my lines were in disarray. *OK*, I thought. *I'll just have to get used to it.* I had tried everything I knew. I had apologized, complained, ignored, avoided and still we were at odds.

As I set my gear on the dock and prepared to board the boat I noticed something strange. My boat had a stain – a yellow stain. When I looked closer, I realized that someone had urinated on my boat!

That was the last straw. I no longer felt safe there. What would be next, sugar in the gas tank? I was shaking when I called Ariel on the phone to tell her about the latest in this ongoing saga between Dick and me. We both agreed it was time to bring *Dream On* home because the dream had turned into a nightmare.

For two weeks our boat resided in the boat barn beside our house. I called Zuley and told her to rent my slip to someone else, I could no longer abide going to her marina. At night, the situation would gnaw on me before sleep. Then suddenly, the answer to my puzzling, distressing situation came to me. I knew what I had to do: I needed to apologize, really apologize.

Yes, I had told Dick I was sorry before, but it was to get what I wanted – to get him off my back, out of my hair, away from my boat. I woke up at 4 A.M. realizing that Dick takes great pride in his job, his abilities and responsibilities and I had rebuffed him way back when I wouldn't let him help me with my docking that day. Everything else had grown from this moment. I could be "Right" or I could be "Alive."

Ariel and I often talk with people about the difference between being right and being alive, and that to be right, even if you are accurate, there is a cost. You have to give up being alive. And if you want to experience being alive, you have to give up being "right." I knew that I was right that Dick shouldn't be messing with my boat, but I could maintain that stance or really, truly make peace.

I woke up Ariel to tell her about my realization. "I know what to do, Ariel. I need to apologize to Dick and really mean it. I need to go there, with my heart open, and apologize for real, whether he accepts it or not. I hurt his feelings. I was unkind. I need to make amends."

"I'm glad," she said sleepily, throwing her arm over my chest. "How about we go down there tomorrow? Let's pick him up some local peaches at the farm next door as a gift."

The next day, we got a half-bushel of peaches and hitched up the boat and trailer to our Suburban and headed down to Zuley's. It was a hot day and when we arrived Dick was standing on the dock, talking with a friend. I took a deep breath and got out of the car. Resting the box of peaches on her hip, Ariel accompanied me on my mission.

Dick glared at me as I walked up. I said to him "Dick, I'd like to talk with you, I really owe you an apology." With a surprised look, Dick's friend walked away, giving us privacy. Dick appeared shocked and skeptical, but I continued.

"I behaved like a horse's behind and I'm really sorry for all the grief I've caused you with Zuley. I know you're doing a great job around here and the last thing you need is someone like me giving you grief. I would really appreciate it if you would accept my apology."

"You know," he said. "It takes a big man to admit when he's wrong." And he extended his big hand. I clasped it and he gave me a firm shake. "You should have told me you had permission to be on the dock that time. I would have understood."

I realized then that Dick didn't remember the originating event. He didn't even remember how, in his opinion, I had snubbed him. His memory of events was different than mine. I knew I could tell him that I *had* told him I had permission to be on that dock, but he hadn't wanted to listen. I knew it was the truth, but I also knew that it would just reignite the fires of unrest and I was ready for peace.

"You're right, Dick." I said. "Again, I'm sorry."

"Forget it," he replied.

I took the box from Ariel. She had been a witness to the event and was quietly holding the gift. If he had rejected my apology we would have taken the peaches back home because they were truly meant as a gift and not as a pay-off to facilitate a truce. "Our neighbor grows the most delicious peaches. These are for you."

Dick took the box. He put them on the front seat of his car and told us his girlfriend would make some pies. We asked him where he would like us to park once we put our boat in the water and he indicated a place. For the first time in two years, we went down to our boat fully at peace with Dick and the boatyard.

A funny thing happened for the rest of that season. Our lines remained neatly coiled on the dock and I didn't have to screw them down anymore. I imagine Dick's pie tasted very sweet.

13

WHO ARE YOU REALLY PUNISHING?

*I*t has been said that we have close to 200,000 thoughts a day and that 98 percent of those thoughts are repeats of the day before and the day before that. Our minds are machines that embellish upon past thoughts to prove ourselves right about our point of view about what happened in the past.

When growing up, our parents were the authority figures, the boss, the person or people who told us when to go to bed, when to eat, when to turn off the television, when to do our homework, etc. Sometimes we agreed with our parents. Most of the time, however, we defined our independence in opposition to them. The problem is, if you believe that your parents "did you wrong," then anyone who in any way appears similar to the authoritarian figures we called parents will trigger mechanical ways of relating in us that are not in our best interests, but since they are mechanical they're automatic.

We are suggesting a new and unique possibility: to complete one's past by letting go of the stories we have concocted and embellished over time. These stories, may we remind you, were recorded from the point of view of who you were at the time of the alleged incidents. You may believe them to be true but it doesn't mean they are.

Here is an example:

A successful businessman named Bob asked to have a private consulting session with us. He was upset that his ability to relate with women was such a challenge that his marriage had quickly fallen apart and ended in a messy divorce and now his current relationship with his girlfriend seemed to be heading in a similar direction. Once we sat down together, he immediately launched into what he felt was the reason for his failed relationships. It was his mother's fault. He knew it. Without prompting he told us a graphic story about how his mother had tortured him as a little boy.

"She picked me up and sat me down on a hot stove," he said.

"I want to see the scars," Shya replied.

Suddenly Bob became still. His face got a faraway look as if re-running the scene in his mind's eye. Then the story changed.

"I *thought* it was going to be hot," he said.

We gently smiled in response.

Bob took another breath and sat for another moment.

"It was warm," he eventually admitted. "I was scared."

Bob was a man of about sixty years of age who had truly believed the lie he told himself when he was five or six and it had dominated his life and his ability to have nurturing relationships ever since.

We don't know what eventually became of Bob. But we have seen over and over that if you want to have what is possible in life, you need to let go of the past – whether real or imagined. When you hold onto a vendetta with someone, you bring that story forward in time and you impose the past on the present. When you are determined to prove that your mother or father, for instance, hurt you, then you can't let your life fully flower because then they wouldn't have done such a "bad" job after all. When you punish another person by feeling bad, the person you actually punish is you.

MEMORIES: THE HOME OF THE WHOPPER (AS TOLD BY SHYA)

"I've experienced many terrible things in my life, a few of which actually happened." – Mark Twain

I told some whoppers when I was a kid. Some were childish phantasmagorical imaginings – like those of my grandson Max when he was five years old. Once Max and I were playing in the yard and he found a worm. He held it up for my inspection and with conviction announced that worms have 100 brains and that is why it is good to eat a worm's head. I asked him how he knew this and he replied, "Timmy told me and he knows everything." Max's friend was seven years old but to Max's young and immature perspective, Timmy was an expert whose stories were not stories to be questioned, but facts.

Some of the fibs I told in my youth were calculating and unkind, though I wasn't fully aware of it then. Like the time I told my mother an entirely fabricated story that I had been harassed on the way home by a band of older bullies who called me names – all in an elaborate attempt at misdirection so that she would be so concerned with my welfare that she wouldn't notice that I had slipped a couple of dollars from her pocketbook.

But of all the tales I told, large and small, I hardly expected that a whopper of a fish tale would come back to me more than fifty years later from the memory of a child, now a man.

When I was in my early teens, a fellow named Marvin Victor worked for my Dad and Marvin and I shared a mutual interest in fishing. So although I was young, he and I started a friendship that lasted well into my adulthood until he ultimately died from a failed kidney transplant. When I was a youngster, Marvin would take me bass fishing in upstate New York. He also had a stepson, Mark, who was three or four years younger than I so he encouraged us to be friends. I tried to be friendly, of course, but like most fifteen-year-olds, a boy of eleven or twelve wasn't of much interest. Mark looked up to me, though. He trailed after me as boys are wont to do and I told him a fish story or two about "the ones that got away" – or in my case, a really good fantasy about the one that got blown up.

My vivid imagination was a fertile ground for stories of daring and excitement that in fact had never happened. So I told Mark in great detail about the time I caught a really large striped bass one day while fishing. But, according to my story, instead of letting the bass go or keeping him for dinner I took a cherry bomb (a really large firecracker), lit the fuse, stuffed it down the fish's gullet and let him swim down to the murky deep. The fish, I said, ultimately exploded in a spray of water and fish guts and slime and scales. I can almost see it now.

Mark, a wide-eyed youth, believed my tale. Of course, that is just what I'd intended. Just like telling ghost stories and shouting "Boo!" was supposed to scare my friends, which it always did, even if they knew what was coming.

Some fifty years later, Mark and I reconnected. He was now a father of two children of his own. As we spoke, it quickly became apparent that he was bristling with anger toward his father and stepfather for things that he remembered happening during his childhood. Oddly enough, given his vitriol toward his own dad and stepdad, Mark was now a psychologist and, as a family therapist, he made a practice of helping other people move on in their own lives.

As Mark and I casually chatted about our childhoods, a funny thing happened. He brought up the exploding bass story and it quickly became obvious that his childish mind had rewritten the fable as if it were true. He not only believed I had demolished that fish, he now even remembered the story as if he'd been there actually watching the event. It was a larger-than-life lie reconfigured as truth.

Gently I tried to tell him it wasn't true. He was highly insulted. It was as if I had told a man in his early sixties that the Santa he believed in all these years was a myth. He tenaciously held onto his memories even though as a psychologist he knew that studies have proven how false memories can be remembered even more vividly than actual events.

I mentioned the studies to Mark and although he knew of them he swore it wasn't true in his case and, after momentarily being taken aback by his vehemence, I could quickly see the difficulty. If Mark challenged this long-held and treasured memory it would open up Pandora's box. If he admitted to the possibility that his memory was faulty, then what about the list of grievances against those who raised him that he still held as viable and true? What would happen if all of that fell away and he had to look at the possibility that he was simply angry, and that his anger wasn't caused by his dad, or his childhood or any of the other really good reasons he gave himself? What if his world was built on childish whoppers rewritten as reality over time?

Occasionally my current circumstances trigger old memories of times I was "done wrong" as a child. But now I can actually smile as I realize that some of these events probably never happened. And even if they did, my remembrances need hold no sway over my life today.

They are just old ghost stories and I no longer need to jump when those memories say "Boo!" Or even when they say "Boo Hoo!"

THE BLAME GAME

We have been trained in the culture we grew up in to blame the current circumstances of our lives – including how we feel, and whether or not we are "successful" – on our past. We have been taught to blame other people, particularly our parents, and how they treated us in the past, for any of our current complaints or perceived failings. Our parents have become the "go to" scapegoats for anything and everything that we judge about ourselves.

But, as we have seen in the previous section, the memories of our past, upon which most of us base our current reality, may be flawed. If you give up your right to be right that another person or events from the past are responsible for how you are being in *this* moment, then you have the possibility of having your own life. But as long as you are committed to blaming your past (and your parents) for how you are today, then you will replay the same scenarios over and over again.

14

IF YOU GET UPSET,
TRY SAYING "YES!"

*P*eople often erroneously think that once they wake up, transform, have an enlightening event or series of events that they will never get upset again. There is also a misconception that years of looking at your life buys you something and that you should have permanent relief from getting disturbed.

Getting upset is not a failing, but to the mind that wishes to "get somewhere," the mind that wishes to achieve enlightenment, it is.

Have you ever said to yourself:

I thought I was over that already
I don't like being upset
I hate this
I don't wanna be upset

Those thoughts are all about resisting this moment of now and being a No to how your life is showing up.

Most of us have the idea that enlightenment and transformation will save us from the domination of our lives. We think that if we become enlightened we'll have power over sickness, fatigue and getting upset. So we strive to calm our minds, quiet the voice in our heads and gain control over our environment.

Here is the good news and the bad news: You have no control over how life shows up. It's bad news if you're trying to be in control because life doesn't really care what you want. ***The good news is that you can discover how to be a Yes to how your life is unfolding in the moment and then miraculously, disturbing forces cease to disturb.*** The paradox is that you have no control, yet when you are a Yes to your life, you have ultimate control because what is happening becomes your choice. But you can't *do* being a Yes in order to be in control. In other words, if you pretend to be a Yes but really are attempting to change the circumstances to meet your preferences or if you manipulate yourself or others to get what you want, then you are actually being a No in disguise.

We all have the idea that when we get enlightened, we will no longer be affected by circumstances and our current environment, that we will somehow be independent of the culture of which we are a part. Yet, our environment affects us. We feel other people's disturbances and if we resist them, we become what we resist: disturbed.

It is likely that you are reading this book, in part, hoping to stop getting upset and being disturbed. But you can still be triggered, especially if you resist something. When you resist something like a body sensation, a thought, or an unwanted emotion, you push against it. Once you resist something, you become what you resist. With awareness, you can train yourself to be a Yes to this moment, however it is showing up. This includes being a Yes to your upset if you feel disturbed. ***Being upset is not a failure. You can simply notice it and move on. Simply seeing that you are upset without judging yourself is enough for it to dissolve.***

GRAVITY: THE GREATEST TEACHER

If you want to learn to approach things with awareness, a nonjudgmental way of being, then gravity is the greatest teacher. It's never angry. It's never frustrated with you when you fall off balance. It's implacable, impartial, relentless and uncompromising. You can't pacify gravity by being on good behavior. Gravity is never sentimental. It doesn't say, "Oh, Johnny was so good today, I think I will let this little tipping-over episode go – I'll pull him to the ground on another day." Gravity also doesn't get hurt feelings or feel bad when you take a tumble. It doesn't care if you have a temper tantrum and cry when you fall. Gravity isn't positive or negative. It is consistent and indifferent to your reaction to it. It just keeps teaching until you learn how to maintain your balance.

Gravity also doesn't remember yesterday. It doesn't keep a list of your "wrongdoings" and punish you for them over time. If you are upright and on balance today, it doesn't pull you over to get even for some supposed slight in the past. It isn't apologetic for being itself. It doesn't say, "I am so sorry, Suzy, for having to pull you over today – really I am." Gravity just is. And because it is, you can count on it.

It is not too late to keep learning from gravity. You can learn to be consistent, and see your actions in a neutral, nonjudgmental manner without adding that extraneous internal conversation that comments about what you have done – a conversation that adds agreement to or finds fault with your way of being.

How often have you berated yourself over time for something you did "wrong"? If you make a misstep and trip, or if you stub your toe gravity will never tell you that you are "clumsy" or "stupid."

You fell often when you learned to walk – you just don't remember it. And interestingly enough you learned to walk without having to make decisions or having to talk with yourself about your actions. You walked without having to make a resolution about how to be a better you. You walked without having to remember anything and without rehashing in your mind everything that led up to landing on the ground. You learned organically. Learning to walk and the lessons of gravity have stayed with you and yet you have no resentment toward it and little or no memory of it. Gravity truly is the greatest teacher.

WHEN OLD HABITS RE-EMERGE – THINK PEPPERMINT!

Are you proud that you no longer lose your temper, bite your fingernails, or have a messy desk? Perhaps you feel that you have finally arrived since you no longer wait until the last minute to do things. Did you ever think you were finished with a pesky old habit and then unexpectedly find it was still there? You thought you kicked a habit once and for all and suddenly, for no apparent reason, you are nibbling those nails or procrastinating once again? Bummed when it happens? Don't worry – Think peppermint!

In the '90s, the two of us rented a little cottage in Woodstock, New York, where we had a large deck with southern exposure. One summer, we built wooden planters that were six feet long by two feet wide that we filled with rich soil. Then we planted a range of vegetables and herbs in them: tomatoes, zucchini, summer squash, lettuce and arugula. We also planted dill, cilantro, oregano, thyme and marjoram. Since we wanted to make iced tea with sprigs of fresh mint, we also planted one small peppermint plant in the corner of one of the long boxes but we didn't know the properties of mint.

Peppermint plants not only grow up and out above the ground, they do the same thing underground. All healthy plants put down roots but peppermint puts down rhizomes, thick white stems that grow sideways, only to pop up a distance away, masquerading as whole new plants. It wasn't so much of a problem at first. A little extra peppermint here or there was fairly easy to weed. But we didn't realize that while we were pulling out the plant above ground, the roots were virtually impossible to pull. These hardy creepers ranged far and wide and grew until we had new little plants popping up in the midst of all of our other herbs. We pulled what we could but the rootstock is robust and it winters over very well.

After harvesting at the end of the season, we dumped all the planters in one pile in a nearby field. The next spring, we mixed in compost and fertilizer and refilled the planters, replacing them on our deck with fresh plants and seeds for a new season.

As things began to sprout and grow, suddenly we had peppermint – everywhere. We hadn't realized that while the plant died back, the roots did not and when we chopped up the soil, we also chopped the remaining rhizomes and each little slice of rootstock became a viable plant. For the rest of the time that we had those planters, peppermint became a matter of maintenance, not eradication.

By now, most of your "bad" habits are well-developed rootstock. When you get engaged, on board, enlivened about your life, these habits go dormant. But the ground is fertile and those roots are still viable. No need to be discouraged or feel like you "haven't gotten anywhere" when your personal peppermint pops up its minty little head. Weed it! Nip those young leaves in the bud. Get back to work. Re-engage. Judging yourself for your bad habits' regenerating is like adding a big fat dose of Miracle-Gro®. However, approaching those habits with awareness – a nonjudgmental seeing – acts like a natural pesky-cide. It neutralizes those pesky ol' habits so you can grow what you want in your garden and not be plagued by your old roots.

15

YOUR THOUGHTS ARE NOT YOU

*M*ost people identify themselves with what they are thinking. So if they think, "I am right about this," then they believe it to be true. Have you ever been upset and sure of your position that "you" are right and "they" are wrong, only to calm down and discover that your internal conversation was all a part of being agitated?

If you want to be clear about what is a thought and what is "you," it's simple. Any sentence that you say to yourself containing the word "I" is a thought:

I like / I don't like
I don't understand
I can't
I want
I won't
I am

Most people think that they are their thoughts. They believe that the voice they listen to, the voice that speaks to them about how they are doing, about how life is showing up, what they want or don't want, is really them. They don't think that they are listening to some disembodied commentary, one that is sometimes accurate and sometimes not.

Until you discover the possibility that you are not your thoughts as a context from which to live life, you are forever believing that that voice is you and what it says is true to your experience. And it isn't. Sometimes, the voice will say, *I'm hungry*, when you have finished a sumptuous meal. Sometimes it will say, *I'm tired*, when you are full of energy. Most of what the voice does is complain about you or your current circumstances and how something else will be better than what you have. You are not your voice. ***You have a voice. And when you can make the distinction between the one who listens and the voice, you get control over the mechanical nature of life.***

THE WIRELESS INTERNET OF YOUR MIND
Do you realize that you influence your environment and your environment influences you? Did it ever occur to you that your mind is a sophisticated wireless sender and receiver of thoughts, knowledge and information? Have you ever had the experience of thinking about someone and they call or text you shortly thereafter, or of thinking about something and then you receive a letter or an email about it?

For example, parents famously develop an uncanny ability to "know" when to check on their children. In infancy, when a child is helpless, parents develop a sixth sense for when their offspring are in need. When children are playing and things get "too quiet," that's a cue for a parent to make sure the kids aren't getting into mischief. Later in life, parents often retain that uncanny ability to call at "just the right time" or hone in on subjects that a grown child is trying to avoid.

Have you begun investigating the wireless capabilities of your mind, your ability to connect into and be in sync with your environment? Below are two experiences of this phenomenon – one from Ariel's perspective and one from Shya's.

LOST LAKE (AS TOLD BY ARIEL)
When I was a child, there was a television show called *Kreskin's ESP*. Our family watched an episode one night when Mike, a fellow from our hometown, was featured. He had gone to a taping the previous spring and had decided to test Kreskin. After writing down the name of a place in Oregon, *Lost Lake*, on a piece of paper, Mike had folded it up and slipped it into his pocket. This way, Mike explained, he would have tangible proof if the Amazing Kreskin came up with these words. As the show progressed, Kreskin demonstrated his ability to tune in to the audience. At one point he said, "Lost Lake. I'm hearing 'Lost Lake.'" I was very impressed that Kreskin had "heard" the words that were hidden in Mike's pocket.

How did Kreskin do it? Quite possibly, he quieted his mind sufficiently that he could hear other people's thoughts. But also key to this ability is that Kreskin didn't identify his thoughts as "him." Most people identify their thoughts as theirs and theirs alone and usually believe that their thoughts are them. For example, if you think, "I don't like this," you think that you don't like this, whatever the "this" is. If you make the basic assumption that your thoughts are you, or that they're private, discreet and yours, you will not be aware of the nuances of your thought patterns. You also will not notice how your way of thinking is impacted by your environment and how your environment is affected by your thoughts.

HOW WILL I PAY FOR IT? (AS TOLD BY SHYA)
As you get more skilled at becoming aware of the fluidity of your thoughts, you may discover that you have a stron-

ger link, a clearer connection with certain people. Over the years, I've had several friends and acquaintances with whom I seem to have a direct conduit and for whatever reason, we occasionally "communicate" at night.

In 2008, when the stock market fell dramatically, Ariel and I didn't have much money tied up in stocks so our financial well-being was not threatened by the decline. However, around this time, I woke up in the middle of the night plagued by a conversation in my head about paying for my children's college education – but I didn't have children of college age any more. However, later that morning, a close friend of mine who lives in a town more than 100 miles away called to tell me he had lain awake the night before, worrying about the stock market and how it would affect his lifestyle. He has two children and at the time, one was a freshman in college and one was in her last year of high school.

As you become aware of the pattern of your thoughts, and as you disengage from the idea that your thoughts are yours alone, you will discover that you no longer have to follow or be dictated to by your inner commentary. Rather, your thoughts become a resource. And just like with the radio, if the station you are listening to is disturbing or no longer interesting, you are free to change the channel.

YOU NEVER WALK THE DOG!
(BEYOND COINCIDENCE)

Do you still think that your private thoughts are private? Do you believe that they are yours and yours alone? Have you seen yet how your environment and the people who are in it can dramatically impact what and how you think?

Let's investigate the phenomenon of linking up with those around you and your interconnectivity to other human beings. Start by becoming aware of your thought processes and internal conversation. Notice the changes in flavor, cadence or content of those thoughts. As you depersonalize what "you" are saying in the apparent privacy of your thoughts, you no longer have to fall prey to your mind's machinations. If you notice your thoughts without judging them, your internal commentary will no longer have to dominate your actions and your life. Who knows? Bringing awareness (a nonjudgmental observing) to your thoughts may even save you from fighting a fight that isn't yours!

The two of us had a dramatic example of this in 1989. It was early in our careers and we were not as firmly rooted in a transformational lifestyle as we are today. It was much easier then to lose our center. On this particular occasion, we were about to give a private consulting session to a couple who were seeing us on the recommendation of a friend. They made the appointment by phone so we hadn't yet met them in person. Arriving a bit early to the apartment we used for our coaching, we made ourselves a cup of tea and suddenly we began to bicker. As our disagreement escalated, it went something like this:

"It would be nice if you'd give me a hand in here." "Don't talk to me in that tone. I've done plenty today." "Yeah? Well, you never help in the kitchen. I'm always doing the dishes." "Yeah? Well, you never walk the dog!"

At that moment, we froze in amazement. We didn't have a dog. In fact, in all the years we'd been together, we'd never had a dog. We burst into laughter and the bickering was busted.

Shortly thereafter, the couple arrived. As we sat together, they began to discuss what they saw as the disconnect in their relationship. They laid out their list of grievances: She doesn't do this, he doesn't do that.

Finally, one of them said it: "Yeah? Well you never walk the dog!"

We looked at each other in amazement. It was a moment beyond coincidence. We knew everyone had the ability to sync up with others, but this was a dynamic demonstration of synchronized thinking that we have never forgotten. It crystallized a possibility that led us to a line of inquiry that is still alive today.

Don't forget, we had never met either of these people in person. The only contact we had was over the phone to set an appointment time. Yet their way of being transcended time and space and somehow we received the essence of them in our own situation and circumstances. So much so that we started acting out their dynamic. You could think of it like someone coming to your home bringing a dish for dinner. As they arrive at your front door, the smell of the food precedes them into your living room and as the aroma wafts into your home it smells as if you have been cooking.

We are not sure *how* it happens. But we are sure *that* it happens. Look around you right now. Think about the air you're breathing. If you looked across the room or off to the horizon, aside from air quality on a hazy day, common sense says that nothing much exists between you and the next hard surface. Now plug in a radio. Turn on a wireless router for your computer. Activate a Bluetooth device or turn on your Smartphone. There is information floating in the air around you and through you. Human beings are the most sophisticated receivers on the planet but science hasn't yet caught up with the measurements and explanation of how it works.

Next time you think, "I don't want to get up," or you find yourself mentally complaining about your job, your relationship, or any other aspect of your life, you don't have to take what "you" are saying so seriously. When you find yourself wanting to hum along with the "I should be farther along in my life by now" tune playing in the background, you can turn your attention to other things. When you find the impulse to bicker, you can relax and bypass that urge. (Yet, if you *do* bicker or find yourself complaining, then this is your responsibility – not whomever you are "in sync" with.)

Feeling well in yourself can communicate across the ethos, too. It's like a telephone line – it goes both ways. You can catch the disturbances that occur around you but others can "catch" your way of being also – including your sense of well-being.

LINKRONIZATION

"Linkronization" is a term we've come up with to describe the phenomenon of linking up and syncing up with another individual or with a group. Think of it like a tuning fork. If a tuning fork is struck, another tuning fork can spontaneously vibrate along with it in a sympathetic resonance.

In our earlier examples, Kreskin was talented at "linkronizing" with his audience and we linked up and synced up with our new clients so completely we had bickered about walking a dog – even though we didn't have one.

Over the years, the two of us have learned how to feel supported by the phenomena of connecting with others rather than feeling disturbed. Like Shya's late night musings about paying for college, we observe our thoughts rather than believe them to be true or ours alone. If our thoughts change cadence or tone before an individual session with a client or prior to leading a course, we notice the changes and hold them as information. Since the second idea of Instantaneous Transformation has to do with the perfection of the moment (You can only be exactly as you are in any given instant), then even grouchy thoughts are perfect, too.

Don't misunderstand us here. If you linkronize with someone in the midst of having a temper tantrum and you start to act out along with him or her, this isn't the fault of the other person. It's your own irresponsibility. However, *if you notice that you have an unkind thought pattern and you see it without judgment, it will wind down or complete itself all on its own.* If you tune in to someone who isn't feeling well in themselves and you allow yourself to be OK and not act out that reality, your way of being can travel back through your wireless linkronization and spontaneously affect the other's sense of him or herself, much like striking a "well-being" tuning fork. However, you cannot "feel well" in order to change another's way of being, as that is a manipulation to advance an agenda.

16

YOU CAN'T DO IT ALONE

*I*ndependence and freedom are the background upon which many of our lives are played. So we may not be making use of our support system of friends around us because we're locked into an unexamined need to prove we can do it alone. If you want to be enlightened, self-realized or live a life that is determined by you rather than by mechanical behaviors that you've learned, it's important to get involved in or create a community of people who are invested in examining their lives and their behaviors. In this way, you can move past the mechanical behaviors you learned to survive towards true independence, which is actually an interdependence with others.

Since it is so difficult to see yourself clearly, a community committed to self-realization and excellence creates an environment in which the members can reach their own potential. Having someone to talk to, to share ideas with, to support you in going for excellence and not quitting on yourself is a rare gift. When you are feeling down and it all seems too hard to continue, those are the moments that a community can support you in rediscovering well-being. It's easy to get discouraged. Life is full of disappointments, but when you realize you're not traveling that road alone, you can keep going. When you're in a community, you realize that you make a difference, that you matter. This supports you in being your true self and supporting others as well, which is truly satisfying. Such was the case with our friend Eric. He came to one of our seminars certain he had nothing "special" to offer and left realizing that simply being himself was a gift.

SIMPLE GIFTS

Although we had been good friends a long time ago, we hadn't seen Eric in more than 20 years. It was the first time he had attended one of our *Say YES to Your Life!* evenings in New York City. He had traveled from Boston to attend our special event, *Employee of the Year,* a seminar devoted to discovering how to bring excellence to the workplace. There were many others attending for the first time that night – most were cautiously optimistic about what was possible, curious about what they might learn.

Eric came to the evening with a plan: Sit back and listen. He thought that would be the best way to approach the seminar since, to his way of thinking, he had nothing of value to offer. Thankfully, his plan failed. Here is what happened:

As we looked out at the faces, we could tell that people were looking for many different things but we felt fairly certain that everyone had an interest in being more successful, productive and satisfied at work. We also knew that most people have internalized standards that they unknowingly compare themselves to and many fall short in their own estimation. So we posed a question: "What attributes do you think embody the Employee of the Year?"

It was an exciting exploration. Many volunteered ideas

– doing complete work with consistency, operating with passion, listening, being responsive to your colleagues and customers, as well as many other useful suggestions. Each attribute someone brought forward came to life as people passionately articulated how they felt and what they saw.

Suddenly, a man in the front row stood up. "I'm not sure what my idea of Employee of the Year was before I came in here tonight," he said, "but being passionate about your job just leapt to the top of my list."

The evening was heating up and, like popcorn, suddenly Eric blossomed and popped out of his chair to add his voice. "I live in Boston and New York City," he told everyone, "and I take a really nice bus between the two that has an Internet connection. I had a plan this week to do research work via the Internet on the bus on the way down from Boston, but the bus broke down. First I was upset, but that didn't make the bus move. Then I texted my complaints to my friends, but that didn't make the bus move either."

People chuckled as they relaxed into the evening and Eric's story. He went on to say that he had been listening to our podcasts and had our first book, *Working on Yourself Doesn't Work: The Three Simple Ideas That Will Instantaneously Transform Your Life*, with him. In an instant, while "stuck" on a bus, he had a direct experience of the Second Principle of Instantaneous Transformation: He could only be exactly where he was. That *this* was his moment. Complaining wouldn't change the fact that the bus had broken down. So he quit complaining and got engaged, chatting with people around him, looking out the window. Eric grinned as he told everyone that he made a couple of new friends that day. He had surprised himself by entertaining those around him.

The evening continued and it was lively, informative and inspired as the diverse group of participants gave each other many gifts, simple stories such as Eric's. At the end of the evening a young man named Bill who had been a silent observer over the course of the night approached us to say that he had been pleasantly surprised to discover that he wasn't alone – that he'd been able to relate to all of the people who'd spoken. He let us know that he had been looking at improving the quality of his life for some time now but had felt like he was in possession of only fragmented ideas. Now it was as if those fragments unexpectedly and effortlessly fit together into a usable form.

"It wasn't all new," Bill said. "But suddenly I felt OK in myself. The best part was when that man Eric spoke about his experience on the bus. I really understood it. I saw that I can only be where I am – but it is up to me what I do with it."

As we interacted with Bill, we couldn't help but smile. Saying Yes to your life is so simple, yet the results are so profound. In a moment your life can transform and a whole new world, an entirely new possibility, is open and available.

We are so happy that Eric failed in his plan to keep quiet. His failure was a win, not only for himself but also for everyone, including a rather shy young man named Bill.

We know Eric came to the evening with the misconception that he had nothing of value to contribute. He had no idea that the spontaneous sharing of his experience would make such a difference. People absolutely underestimate what they have to offer. We pre-judge ourselves, thinking we are damaged or "works in progress" or that our "ordinary lives" are nothing special.

We love that Eric and many of the folks there that evening gave themselves permission to be self-expressive even if they thought what they had to say was not of use or at best "ordinary." ***Each person's "ordinary" is another's "extraordinary." Being one's self and sharing that with others is simply a gift.***

17

KINDNESS IS KEY

In order to be moved by life and have a rekindled sense of wonder, kindness is key. When hearing this, most people mistakenly think that being kind to others is what it's about, when really it all starts with being kind to yourself – if you don't have compassion for your own foibles, you won't have it for anyone else's.

Being kind to yourself is a skill set you can learn, much like the skill set of listening. It's about noticing your internal dialogue, the conversation that you have been listening to and believing to be you and not judging that dialogue for its content or tone. If you take a moment to notice the way you talk about yourself in your thoughts, you will notice that you would never be so harsh with another as you are with yourself.

Most people have been taught that they need to be strict or harsh or demanding of themselves in order to produce positive results in any endeavor, but is that really true? Are you more responsive to someone who is kind to you than you are to someone who is cruel and demanding? If you look and are honest, you will probably discover that a little bit of kindness goes a long way to securing your allegiance, your dedication, your support and your loyalty. Being kind to yourself also allows you to recognize and be moved by the greatness in others.

I CAME FACE-TO-FACE WITH GOD AND WAS HUMBLED (AS TOLD BY ARIEL)

The night I came face-to-face with God was sweet and yet ordinary enough. It had been one of those glorious, high-pressure Indian summer days in September and Shya and I decided that after our work was done we would head to the Delaware River and walk across the bridge that connects Lambertville, New Jersey, to New Hope, Pennsylvania.

The sun had dipped toward the horizon as Shya and I strolled hand-in-hand across the bridge. The late afternoon light cut through the river, spotlighting giant carp in the quiet water directly behind each bridge abutment. Swimming, flashing, digging in the mud, hanging motionless as if suspended, there were hundreds of fish, large and small. Like kids, it was hard to contain our excitement. "Oh look," I said pointing to a huge one, "That fish must weigh thirty pounds!"

As twilight descended, we both became hungry and rather than head home, we decided to go to a little Indian restaurant I had noticed on an earlier visit to New Hope. We've found Indian food where we work in New York City or Cambridge, England, and even in Hamburg, Germany, but we had yet to find a place near our home. I was hopeful this establishment would be a place to have a tasty meal.

We took our time, looking in store windows, and eventually came to the tiny restaurant. Stepping inside, we walked down the two steps at the entrance and to our right were several tables, one occupied by four people. Giving them a bit of space, we chose a table against the wall. The owner brought us bright orange paper menus and as we perused them, the other patrons paid their bill and left.

After ordering our meals we were served appetizers of papadum – thin crispy wafers made of lentils – and a condiment tray with three small bowls – a curried yogurt, marinated onions and a tamarind sauce. As we nibbled and dipped, the outer door opened and a couple came in. At first glance I thought they might be indigent, as the man appeared so unkempt with shaggy dark curls and a scruffy patchwork beard. We watched as the fellow, followed by the gal, navigated the steps. He was large and overweight, doughy in appearance and it was obvious that walking was difficult for him. As he descended the stairs, he placed his hand on a little buffet table for balance, sending dishes clattering and a lid flying. His companion, a blonde-haired woman in her late twenties, barked out an embarrassed laugh at the noise.

Initially the couple selected a table in the corner but his considerable bulk made it difficult to fit so the owner respectfully moved their place settings and water glasses to a more comfortable table directly across from us. The gal studied the menu and she read it out loud, stumbling over words like "tropical" and "mango."

Our entrées came and, the other couple largely forgotten, we began to eat. Savory flavors burst on our tongues, tempered by morsels of basmati rice. In a few minutes, the couple was served their papadum and condiments and she began to shout, "What's in this? This is awesome!" Her delight and wonder at what were obviously novel tastes had the proprietor happily explaining the ingredients in each of the condiment trays.

"Oh wow!" she said. "It'll be a little bit longer before we order. This is only the second time I've eaten Indian food and I want to get it right."

"Take your time," the owner replied, disappearing into the kitchen.

When Shya and I had finished our food, he went up front to pay. I stood to put on my vest and I heard a voice so quiet I almost missed his question.

"Did you enjoy your meal?" the large man asked.

"Yes I did," I replied as I moved to stand near their table.

"What did you have?" he asked, tilting his head to look up at me.

"My husband had lamb Vindaloo," I said, aware that they hadn't chosen their meals yet. "It's pretty spicy. I had lamb Rogan Josh which is milder and made with onions and tomatoes."

"I had Indian food once before," the young woman said earnestly, "and they said that the dish wasn't spicy but I tasted one drop on the tip of my finger – one drop, and my mouth was on fire. If that wasn't spicy, I don't know what was! I never want to experience that again."

I was struck by her innocence. She was so unworldly, unsophisticated and simple, just being herself, having a lively conversation with an interested stranger. No self-judgments. No second-guessing. Just being. Just there. It was a sweet moment of connection, one worth savoring.

Then the shaggy-haired man tipped his head back further and suddenly we were face-to-face. I can't say he looked me in the eye as his eyes didn't focus in a proper manner – one eye looked hither, the other yon. His features were diffuse, asymmetrical, round and soft. Quietly he spoke again and I had to strain to hear.

"Have a nice night," he said, and time halted for a moment. In an instant, there was no forward momentum – no need to get somewhere. There was also no past – no history connecting this gentle giant and me. Our spontaneous intimacy was clearly not something built over a lifetime of shared experiences and common interests. Yet his words leapt straight to my heart as this big shaggy bear of a man had no social veneer over his features, no barrier between his heart and mine. Stunned, I was clear that I had just come face-to-face with God.

"Thank you, I really appreciate that," I said as I stood a little straighter and I truly meant it. It's hard to describe how profoundly moved I was by that brief interaction. All potential judgments about appearance, intelligence, education, weight and infirmities were swept aside and for whatever reason, I had met the God inside the man, residing close to the surface, stripped bare of artifice and manipulation. A man not hidden behind his intellect. A man simple, straight and true – a human *being*. It was a humbling experience.

As we left the restaurant and stepped out into the late summer evening, I held Shya's hand and felt truly blessed to be alive.

18

ENLIGHTENMENT IS REVOCABLE

*C*hances are that by now you have experienced enlightenment – at least for moments. You may have even strengthened the skill set of saying Yes to your life with such consistency that you have developed an expanding sense of yourself and sense of well-being. But enlightenment is not a given. It is a moment-to-moment experience and it is revocable. What you have done in the past doesn't buy you anything in this moment. It doesn't matter that you were once calm or that you were once centered. It doesn't matter if in the past you were kind to yourself and compassionate with others. ***It only matters how you are being Right Now.*** Here is an example as told by Shya:

I was sitting in the haircutting chair when David, the salon owner who was trimming my hair, started complaining. I had met David several years before when I was employed by a company that produced transformational seminars and he was a volunteer. He had worked his way up through the ranks of volunteers until he had become a leader of seminars and each week he stood in front of hundreds of people conducting courses designed to support them in having a better quality of life.

As David cut my hair he began complaining about his wife, his career, his life. Eventually I spoke up.

"David," I said, "Stop complaining. You'll feel much better."

Incensed, he quickly replied, "Shya, you are not giving me credit for all the work I've done."

"Yes," I said, "That's true. What you've done and learned doesn't matter. It's of no value if you're not living it right now. How are you being right now? That's all that matters."

David had fallen into the habit of *thinking* that he was clear. He didn't bring awareness to what he was doing and how he was being. As a result, his internal complaints became "truths" and he thought that he was superior to the people about whom he was complaining. Many people who step upon the path of self-discovery fall into the trap of complaining about all those who are not as "evolved" as they are.

When you find yourself complaining you can be sure that you are resisting something and that you are being right about your point of view. **Saying Yes to your life is not a one-time thing.** It's not a pill that you take and then your life is sorted out forever. Life keeps unfolding and in any given moment you can say Yes or No. You can meet it or resist it. You can be the author of your life or the victim. The moment you notice you've been operating as if you're the victim of circumstance, if you don't judge yourself for having been that way, you are centered again. It is as simple as that. It only takes an instant for your life to transform.

19

BEING OF SERVICE

"I don't know what your destiny will be, but one thing I know: the only ones among you who will be really happy are those who will have sought and found how to serve."
– Albert Schweitzer

Laurie showed up with a spring in her step and a noticeably lighter demeanor. There had been a festival in town and she had taken part. In actuality, she had seen little of the entertainment, nor had she partaken of the rides and activities. Instead, she was "in charge of beans." The gathering was a community outreach project produced by her church and she had spent the day at the outdoor barbecue serving beans. We could tell that she came away well-fed.

There are infinite possibilities for service. In your own community there are bound to be plenty of pre-existing avenues or you can create some of your own. Throughout the world there is a grass roots movement to create *Say YES to Your Life!* meetups where people volunteer to lead evenings dedicated to sharing their own experience of Practical Enlightenment, in effect giving it away so that others can have the experience for themselves. The producer of our Internet radio show *Being Here* has selflessly volunteered her time since 2007, making it possible for millions of people to have a taste of Instantaneous Transformation. Teams of volunteers in our transformational community set up our course rooms and manage supplies in order to support others in discovering what is possible for them.

If you want to experience true happiness and well-being in a sustained manner, there comes a time when you must take your attention off your own survival and getting somewhere, and discover how to take care of others and the environment around you. The challenge is that most people think that if they take their attention off their own survival, they won't get what they want or need in life.

Taking care of the people around you supports you in having a brilliant life. But you can't take care of others to get ahead, or to achieve anything. It's got to be a pure act of being of service – not for what you are going to get out of doing it. Here is an example of this as told by Shya:

There was a time, many years ago, when I was managing a group of volunteers at a workshop. As we prepared the room before the seminar participants arrived, there was a couple who were complaining that they had to be there. They had volunteered because, at the time they had agreed to come, somebody had told them that they would get a lot out of assisting (in being of service to others). So they were not assisting to assist, they were assisting to "get" something for what they did. They brought the same complaint they had about other areas of their lives to this project. So I suggested to them that they go home because they didn't really want to be there. I'm sure that when they got home they didn't really want to be there either.

It's funny, when you have your attention on you and how you are doing, for the most part, you're miserable.

Being of service allows you to stop focusing on yourself and striving to get somewhere "better," which is a gift. Since no two things can occupy the same you at the same time, being of service allows you to take your attention off you and the machinations of your mind. Your mind can never be satisfied. Whenever you achieve something or acquire something it automatically races off to want the next thing as if where you are and how you are being is not sufficient, as if you are not already perfect, just as you are. Again, it is all about being here and saying Yes to your life in this moment rather than getting somewhere. But if you take care of others in order to manipulate yourself to be happier or more fulfilled it won't work because in reality, you still have attention on you and how you are doing – the mind is sneaky that way.

RAVING ABOUT COLLEAGUES

"I finally gave away my gold!" Madhu announced one chilly fall *Say YES to Your Life!* evening in Manhattan. Madhu is a man of East Indian descent with mocha-colored skin and luminous brown eyes. In his mid-thirties, he works at a large investment bank, managing aspects of technology that help keep the bank's worldwide systems up and running. Wearing a button-down white shirt under a soft grey cashmere pullover, he stood in front of his audience looking happy and accessible – like the kind of guy you would naturally go to if you had a question about something.

"At the bank where I work we have something called the 'RAVE' system," Madhu said. "RAVE stands for 'Recognizing and Valuing Excellence.' At the beginning of the year each of us are given 12 RAVE awards or 'gold bars' to give away to our colleagues throughout the year to recognize them for outstanding work. When you award someone a RAVE then you submit a short description of how they excelled and they get an email that says, 'You have received a gold bar.' A copy of the RAVE also goes to their manager to make their supervisor aware of the great job he or she is doing."

Madhu turned to us and said with a slightly sheepish grin, "I noticed just the other day that it was already October and I hadn't given out any of my RAVEs. I realized that I was waiting for my colleagues to do something big, important or impressive before I would award them a gold bar. Then I stopped for a moment and really looked at what 'important' means. There are so many things people have done that have dramatically impacted my life in a positive way that I hadn't appreciated. For instance, there is a woman in my department who is in charge of the 'Career Advisors' program where I get to mentor someone fresh out of college. She works behind the scenes and I never really gave her much thought. Then I realized that the young man she paired with me was such a great fit, a pleasure to advise. He really talked to me and listened to my perspective. I found it very rewarding to support him. I easily could have been paired with someone far less compatible. It took nothing for me to stop and recognize my colleague for the great job she is doing and let her know how much I appreciate her. Those 'little' things she does are actually quite big. I discovered that I had been stingy with my praise, which led to a rather cynical, 'sit back and judge others' attitude. When I allow myself to appreciate others around me, then – surprise!" Madhu said. "I suddenly appreciate myself in the process. Wow. I feel great!"

GIVING AWAY THE GOLD
Extending yourself to others so that they, too, can experience well-being is a win/win situation. The more you take your attention away from thoughts like, "How

am I doing?" or "Do I look good?" and direct it toward taking care of the things and people in your environment, the healthier and happier your outlook on life will be. Both Madhu and Eric, who we highlighted in the earlier chapter, "Simple Gifts," thought that they should sit back and listen because they had nothing "special" to offer. Like them, many of us sit back and think about what constitutes "important" things to share. But each person's "normal" can be precious to others. Here's one of our personal examples of giving away the gold:

The days of summer can be rich and warm when the air is crisp, the pressure high and the sunlight filters through the trees in shafts of gold. We love these days. In late July and early August a local farm just down the hill from our home has bushels of summer gold, bright round, sweet, juicy, luscious peaches. We love the smell, the taste and the wonder of a delectable piece of fruit, truly tree-ripened. We like to purchase a small basket of peaches and let it sit out on our kitchen counter. Within a day or two they are so perfectly ripe, we can peel the skin off with our fingers, leaving sensuous flesh ready to slice over cereal and waffles. Or we can just bite into one while leaning over the sink to catch the wild juices. We love summer gold. Peach in hand we realize that we are rich. But poor is the person who keeps great wealth only for him or herself.

We have started a tradition. Each year at the height of the season, we go see Kenny, the farmer who owns the aptly named Tradition Farms, and put in an order for peaches – 60, 100, 120 or so. We get great pleasure from handing someone a perfect peach, sun-ripened summer gold. We search for opportunities to share the wealth. We have been known to bring a large basket to the local State Police barracks and thank them for their service to keep our community and roads safe. We hand them out to the fellows at the garage where we park our car on Mondays and weekends in Manhattan. The men and women who work at the hotel where we hold our seminars always get some, too. Most people know what a peach looks like. Many of us have bought some at the store. But not so many people have had the opportunity to smell and taste a delectable piece of local tree-ripened fruit. The true gift for us is watching someone experience it – often for the first time.

IF YOU WANT TO BE OF SERVICE, START WHERE YOU ARE

Do you have an impulse to volunteer, to step outside of yourself, to make a difference with others? It's easy. Start where you are. Take a look at the things you are passionate about and share them. Take a look at what is going on in your life and know that you are a gift and share that. We have friends who encourage others to accompany them in a full spectrum of activities that they are interested in: "Join me in Hot Yoga," (a great way to ensure that you will exercise, by the way.) "I'm doing a new nutritional program and I am really excited about it. Want to do it with me?" (A great way to spur yourself to keep to your word when dieting). "I found a new coffee bar and I am sure you will love it." Or "I just heard an audio book that you should try."

Look around you. There are many places where you can donate your time and expertise. There are even networking groups, such as BNI – Business Network International, where the foundation of the organization is based on the idea that "Givers Gain®". At BNI, they encourage members to take their attention off themselves and get interested in others. It is about developing meaningful relationships rather than trying to get ahead – about authentically being of service rather than being in survival to grow your business. This organization is a perfect example of doing things to meet your own personal goals while being of service to others.

EMBRACING THE MOMENT

Lenore is an energetic, animated, African-American woman with luminous skin, an ever-changing hairstyle and a keen fashion sense. She came up on stage at one of our seminars fairly vibrating with excitement, which caused the beaded black jacket she was wearing to glitter in the light.

"Hi everyone. My name is Lenore." She began, flashing a smile. "I am so inspired!"

Lenore was standing on the balls of her feet. She leaned toward her audience and, as she did so, her lips began to quiver slightly as her emotions began to overtake her.

"OK, let me slow down," she said and she took a deep breath and regained her center.

None of us knew what she was going to say but she had clearly gotten everyone's attention.

"I wear many hats, so to speak." Lenore began. "I am a sign-language interpreter. Currently I work mainly with students who are in college and I go to their classes with them. I translate what their professors are saying and also translate their questions to the professors."

So saying, she used her hands to demonstrate her words in sign language so we all had the perfect opportunity to really listen with our eyes as well as our ears.

"I also work as a costume designer for films," she continued. "And I am a handbag designer with my own label, Lenorables."

Leaning forward slightly again, her eyes shone passionately.

"Today I had the most wonderful experience at Home Depot. I went in to purchase a number of different things and I had a short window of time to get everything done. As I walked in I noticed an employee who was clearly involved in sorting out various items and handling multiple tasks. I asked him where I could find the first thing on my to-do list. He immediately stopped what he was doing.

"'Go down to the end of this row,' he said, pointing in the direction I needed to go. 'When you get to Aisle 7 turn left. Go about a third of the way down and just after you see the bright blue rolls of masking tape, you'll find what you are looking for on the bottom shelf.'

"It was so precise and so easy. I followed his directions and voila! – I found it immediately. I stood there for a moment amazed by the experience and I thought, *Why hunt around for the things on my list? Why don't I go back to that wonderful man instead?*"

We were all following her words closely. Clearly the ordinary day-to-day event of going to the store had been a memorable occasion.

"So I went back to the first aisle and the guy was still there deeply involved in his project. 'Excuse me,' I said, and I asked him where to find the rest of the items on my list. I was amazed. First of all, he had no hesitancy in answering my questions. He let go of what he was doing and fully took care of me. I didn't have the sense that I was an intrusion or that he was irritated that I took him from his work. Each of his instructions, and where to go to find things and about which aisles they were located in, was as clear and as detailed as his first. So clear, in fact, that I was able to remember what he said and find everything I was looking for in short order.

"I took everything up front and paid. I even headed to the door, ready to step outside when I stopped. *That was remarkable!* I thought. So I went back to the man and asked, 'What's your name?'

"'Bira,' he said.

"When I gave him a quizzical look he even spelled it for me, B-I-R-A," Lenore said while simultaneously signing the letters with her fingers. Her eyes were sparkling as she continued.

"So I told him, 'Thank you, Bira, you have made my day. I found everything. You were great!' and he said, 'Happy to help!'

"As I got ready to leave Home Depot, I somehow felt that I hadn't done enough. I mean, this man was such a great employee, someone just had to know about it. So I went up to the Customer Service desk and asked, 'How do I go about praising an employee who has shown great service today?'

"They told me that there were three ways I could acknowledge someone: Talk to a manager, call an 800 number where I could speak to a representative or I could go online and write a comment.

"So, you know what I did?" She asked us all with a grin. "I did all three!"

Clearly Bira was being where he was. He was being a Yes to the requests that life made of him. He was doing his job as if it was his idea, and interacting with Lenore was not an interruption, but rather a moment that he embraced.

When you go about your day as if what you are doing is perfect, you are being of service and you are a light shining in the world. When you allow yourself to be moved by others and express your gratitude, your light shines even brighter.

20

PERFECTION

It's OK to be excited about your life. It's OK to be wildly enthusiastic about what you are up to. It's also OK if you feel upset. Sometimes people mistakenly think that they have to be in a "good" mood or in the "right" place to be fit to share themselves or to give of themselves to others. Simply taking the attention off your story and how you are doing and giving of yourself pulls you into the moment. If you resist where you are you get lost there. But if you include your current state as though it is perfect, leave it alone and move on, you are free. *This moment is perfect – and so are you.*

ACKNOWLEDGEMENTS

First and foremost we thank Menna van Praag for her lovely foreword and for faithfully shepherding us through the creation of this book. Not only was it fun, the final product is infinitely better for her support and input. Thanks to Andy Gideon for letting us use his "Listening and Its Effect On Learning" article. Andrea Cagan, once again you were a joy to have as our editor and Fernanda Franco your gorgeous cover design and layout are elegant – as are you. Sue Donlon, thanks for being the producer of our Internet radio show, *Being Here* – hard to believe the show has been on the web since 2007. *Being Here* has been part of the backbone for the creation of this work. Thanks also to the talented folks at TAG Online who have gone above and beyond to bring our website to the world – it is not just a job for you but a passion to have transformation be available via the Internet and we are deeply grateful for your partnership. This book would not have been possible without our fabulous support staff, Christina Sayler, Valerie Paik and Leah Schneeflock. Frances Rutherford, we appreciate your meticulousness in the final edits and Bill Sayler, thanks for bringing Ariel's hummingbird to life. Thanks also to all those who have attended our seminars – you are a true source of inspiration. Last but not least, thanks to the courageous folks on the teams in our community – the Setup teams, the ACT team and the ETC team – who work behind the scenes to bring Practical Enlightenment and Instantaneous Transformation to the world. You truly embody "Being of Service."

ABOUT THE AUTHORS

Ariel and Shya Kane are internationally acclaimed seminar leaders, business consultants and the authors of several award-winning books. In 1987, after years of diligently striving to improve themselves and their lives, they spontaneously experienced a profound and fundamental shift. They fell into the current moment, which sparked a new way of living – directly, in this moment of now, without stress, worry or guilt. They have been living this lifestyle and sharing it with others ever since. The Kanes currently lead seminars around the world and host a top-rated Internet radio show, *Being Here.* Their work has been featured in *USA Today, The Huffington Post,* on CBS, ABC and Fox News as well as Sirius XM, NPR and more. Through their approach, millions have discovered how to be productive, effective and satisfied in all areas of their lives without working on their "problems."

There are many ways to connect with Ariel and Shya and be a part of their global community, including their interactive seminars, weekly radio show, blog, email newsletter and social media. To learn more, visit: **www.TransformationMadeEasy.com**